A Glimpse of the Journey

Authored by

Phil Krause

A Glimpse of the Journey

A Review of this book

Phil, I read your book from cover to cover. The forward is true genuine Krause. It obviously comes from the heart.

The early entries were a great insight into your struggles, which I assume are typical of someone on a healthy path of recovery. I can only assume, and I assumed this morning that this book would be helpful to others in the program. While I do not feel that assumption was wrong, I now know it was inadequate.

Your experiences are not only a resource for others in the program, but also offer those who have friends and family struggling with these issues a great insight to the constant struggle you have faced.

Mike Bodine

Preface

When I was a child I formed an idea of what I believed a man to be. Much of this was influenced by television and the adults I was exposed to. My father, his friends like Roger Smith, Clyde Sisson, Bud Morris to name a few, were men who took care of their responsibilities, cared deeply for their families, were strong and confident. These men were my hero's. I hoped to grow up and emulate the men they were.
Somewhere along the way I lost that ideal or I lost interest in it. As my addiction progressed I became less and less of the man I wanted to be and more and more of the person I despised. In the end I would look in the mirror to straighten my hair or trim my beard but I wouldn't look myself in the eye because I hated who I had become.
      This book is a collection of thoughts as I sought and found once again the man I wanted to become as a child. These thoughts were written as text messages that I sent out to the people in my support group and unbeknownst to me collected and saved by my father. My father encouraged me to share them with others in the form of a book and my mother took the time to type them from the hard copies my Dad had collected. I wrestle with putting them in print because they are about personal growth and finding my way back through self-examination. They are deeply personal and originally not meant for anyone but the closest of friends. However my program tells me that I have to share what I have in order to keep it. It is my hope that someone in or seeking recovery may read this and gain some insight into their

own struggles or that perhaps someone watching a loved one struggle may find some understanding of the difficulties of the journey back from the bottom.

Phil Krause

Table of Contents

September 2011 6
October 2011 26
November 2011 56
December 2011 80
January 2012 105
February 2012 123
March 2011 134
April 2012 155
May 2012 165
June 2012 183
July 2012 200
August 2012 210
September 2012 224
October 2012 238
November 2012 245
December 2012 248
January 2013 253
February 2013 256

September 2011

September 11, 2011

Good Morning,

I received this, this morning. It was exactly what I needed to hear.

"Other people's problems may sometimes overwhelm us. But they didn't live this long because of our help. Their problems are not ours even though we feel their pain."

Lately I have been battling with loneliness. The lack of a relationship, the lack of intimacy in my life, not sex, intimacy. That special someone to share your thoughts, hopes and dreams with. What a blessing to have such minor problems in my life. The problems I have now are good problems. No longer do my problems involve such things as the definite ends of jails, institutions and death.

Not to mention I have rooms full of people to have intimate relationships with. Counting blessings, sometimes I lose track, as they come flying at me faster than I can count.

September 12, 2011

Good Morning,

This morning I realized two things, 1) There is a direct correlation between missing meetings and my head not being in the right place and 2) Changes come slowly over a period of time. Yesterday was the second day this week that I didn't catch a meeting and also the second day this week that I had a hum drum kind of day.

I substituted church for a meeting. I enjoyed myself quite a bit, however there is no substitute for spending an hour or so with my people. The clarity you guys bring to my life is paramount to the changes that come slowly over time. Dad came into town Saturday and we had a nice visit including my kids and their friends.

Wasn't long ago, that idea would have been pushed aside for other activities. I oh, so much prefer and appreciate the time I get to spend with friends and family now.

Got a little carried away this morning, 90n90 get a sponsor.

Ride the turtle,

Phil

A Glimpse of the Journey

September 13, 2011

Good Morning,

Read the reading and figured I had better share this. I have been having "using" dreams like crazy lately. They used to not bother me, aside from waking up feeling guilty when I first woke (I hate that feeling). I have been having so many that I am beginning to worry it is a relapse in the making.

So like most of my problems I feel the need to share and hear what you all have to say. Things that are going on in my life that swirl around in my head are, still some resentment towards the estranged and her boyfriend, school has been keeping me crazy busy, the lack of a relationship has been bothering me some and I haven't made time to speak with my sponsor lately either. Have a speech I am doing today that I am a bit nervous about. Big class project going on in business principles and the list goes on and on. May just be a bit overwhelmed. But I know this is where the fixing starts for me, with all of you. The people I know, know me. Love.

Fwd: So I sent out that text, within thirty minutes five people had texted me back. Darren called and as I am talking to Darren big Rick knocks on my door at 5:45 a.m.

Get the feeling I have good friends.

September 14, 2011

Julie decided to keep the kids last night. I miss them when they are gone, but am happy that they are getting to see their Mom more.

I keep seeing changes in me that I like. Yesterday I spent several hours working on a project for Business Principles with a classmate. Had a blast doing homework.

Homework a blast? Who Is this guy and what have they done with Phil?

Slowly over a period of time. All this way in 10 months. Well worth the wait. Keeps getting better.

You NA people are sneaky. Keep healing me when I'm not looking. I've got my eyes on you now, and my ears, and my mind. Keep it up. I'm listening.

Love,
Phil

September 15, 2011

Good Morning,

This is going to be a short one. I woke feeling grateful for the friends I have. What a group of misfits and addicts. I feel sorry for those who aren't. They are missing out on the most loyal, caring and loving people I have ever met. I love you all. Each and everyone of you.

Ride the turtle.

Phil

September 16, 2011

Good Morning,

Yesterday I was reminded that I can carry the message but not the addict. To watch someone you love with all your heart not get it is heartbreaking. I still look and see this person suffering and think, "you have no idea what you're missing." But I have to remember that from their point of view they are probably looking me thinking, "you have no idea what you are missing."

It was and still is hard for me to remember that I have to let them make up their minds, just because I love them and want what I view as the best for them doesn't mean it's what they should want. They have to decide what's best for them. I have to decide what's best for me. I have a responsibility to myself and my children to do what is best for us. If they want to be a part of that, or apart from that, is up to them. Love you all.

Ride the turtle.

Phil

A Glimpse of the Journey

September 11, 2011

Good Morning,

Something I read this morning hit me as something I needed to share, so short and sweet here it is. "God does not save us from temptation – he sustains us in the midst of them." When I read that it hit me that the word temptation could be easily replaced with so many other words as well: problems, sorrow, even happiness and joy.

My HP sustains me all the time. Through the good and the bad. So much of the time he sustains me through all of you.

Love

September 18, 2011

Good Morning,

I read in one of my readings a line that struck me as one to share. It read something along the lines of "to resist temptation without giving in is a true testament to the growth of good spiritual principles". I truly enjoy waking up in the morning feeling good about what I did yesterday. It gives hope and drive to wake up tomorrow feeling the same way. I love this new life.

I love the relationships new and old that are flourishing in it. Just as the common factor in all the bad things that happened in my life was me, the common factor to all the good that happens in my life is also me. I like the good much more than the bad.

Love to all.

Ride the Turtle.

Phil

September 19, 2011

Good Morning,

Yesterday my ability to parent my children well was brought into question by someone from my past. My first reaction was pain followed immediately by anger. That lasted for a short period of time. Then with the help of two great friends, all the things I have learned in the program and the people in it kicked in. Peace settled over me and I realized that this person knows so little about me now and their opinion is based on anger and resentments from our past.

God does not give us more than we can handle. My clown suit was right there at my finger tips and I chose to let her take center stage at the circus. My act was not required. Thank you all for the things you have taught me and thank those two for being there. Love you all. Ride the turtle and have a great day. Phil

Phil Krause

September 20, 2011

Goooooo Slackers!

Back to bed for an hour or so. Love you all.

Have a turtle riding, 90n90, workin' the steps kinda day.

Phil

A Glimpse of the Journey

September 21, 2011

Good Morning,

Having faith is on my mind this morning. Eleven months ago I had little to no faith. I did have desire to stop using though. That desire was all I needed to start looking for another way, which lit a small fire of belief. Belief that if I stayed clean, I could do better. Doing better wasn't enough to build faith though. Wanting better helped find a meeting. That meeting brought me to all of you people.

That is where I found faith. Seeing people who were doing what I didn't think I could do. That little spark is still fanned by all of you and now sustains me. Thank you all for showing me the way. My faith in this program is because of you. That faith continues to grow as I keep doing things I couldn't do alone.

Love you all. Have a great turtle riding day.

Phil

September 22, 2011

Good Morning,

Funny how honesty works so well in letting me know where I stand with people. It clears the air. When I am honest with other people it clears up many doubts. When I am honest and straight forward, people can base their opinions of me without fear of hidden agendas. I may not like the results. But I know where I stand and can move forward with or without them. I can't expect that I won't get taken advantage of from time to time. But that lasts a much shorter time when I am honest and straight forward.

Love you all.

Rid the turtle,

Phil

September 23, 2011

Good Morning,

Patience is worth the wait. I remember coming in the doors and hearing people talk with such peace in their voices. I couldn't imagine ever getting there. I have been taught many things which have given me the desire to learn more. My mind has been opened which has given me the desire to learn more. My mind has been opened which has given me the desire to be more open-minded. And being honest has given the strength of honesty. Friendships are more friendly.

How blessed I am to have this life. Being able to accept myself has given me acceptance of others.

I see so much room for growth by growing. But instead of being overwhlemed by it, I am inspired. A new perspective on my life. Yeah, to say the least.

Love you all.

Riding the turtle,

Phil

September 24, 2011

Good Morning,

This morning I was awakened by the insanity of recovery and other people dealing with the wreckage of their past and the responsibility of their present. Thank god I was almost up to start my day. Reminded that If I am not careful my life can be crazy whether I am clean or not. I thank those people for that reminder.

I heard yesterday some news I could use to hurt someone and came real close to stirring up the craziness in my life. But the tools I have learned in the rooms kept me on my side of the street. I was very close to starting the insanity of it all over again. I like waking up not feeling bad about what I did yesterday.

Love you all.

Riding the turtle,

Phil

September 25, 2011

Good Morning,

Watching things happen that I don't understand can be so frustrating. It's like watching a fire that has plenty of dry wood, a good base, plenty of heat, a good gentle breeze to coax it along. The fire has everything it needs, but just seems to go out .

Those "whys" are the hardest things to let go of. So I think, is there anything else I could do to make the fire? If so then I must do it. If not then I have done all I can do and it's time to move on. I don't stop caring. But sometimes the fire has to want to burn before it can be lit. And if I sit here waiting for warmth I will die from the cold.

Ride the turtle,

Phil

Phil Krause

September 26, 2011

Good Morning,

I catch myself building things in my head. Whether they be good or bad. For the first several months I was working on my program I was constantly living in the past looking back at the things I had done wrong and building the things into mountains of guilt.

I have accepted those things and I am ok with them. Now I catch myself looking forward and building mountains from nothing, huge shiny objects built of unrealistic expectations. One is just as dangerous as the other.

Looking forward with these grandiose ideas that when they don't come to fruition, disappoint me. Learning to live in the "now" is quite the task for me. Having faith that God is answering my prayers. I just need to do the right things for the right reasons.

Have a great day.

Ride the turtle,

Phil

A Glimpse of the Journey

September 27, 2011

Good Morning,

I am laying in bed looking out the window. It's pitch black outside and I keep thinking to myself, "what a beautiful day". When did this happen? I used to lay here and worry about all the things I had to do. I still have things to do. They will get accomplished. Homework will be turned in on time. Kids won't run out of clean clothes. But those things don't worry me.

Somewhere along the line something happened. This is not a feeling of bliss just a feeling of contentment. Being happy in my own skin.

Love this new life.

Have a great day,

Riding the turtle,

Phil

Phil Krause

September 28, 2011

Good Morning,

Last night I was in class and had an overwhelming need to go to a meeting. So I left class early and went. When I got there I got to attend one of the best meetings I had been to in a while. There were several newcomers there that touched my heart. Reminded me of where I came from and where I never want to be again.

I saw the despair and the confusion, but I also saw hope and desire. I am not a believer in coincidences. Too many amazing things happen in my life for that. When the meeting was over I had a nice conversation with someone I usually don't get along with very well, even gave him a ride and that nice conversation continued in the car.

This life just keeps surprising me. Think I will stick around and see what miracle is next.

Love you all.

Riding the turtle,
Phil

A Glimpse of the Journey

September 29, 2011

Good Morning,

The best of both worlds. This morning I woke with the windows open, the crickets were chirping. It was very peaceful. I was laying there listening and feeling all warm and cozy. Wait warm, ahhh, the windows all open and the heater running its butt off. (Thank god for steady pay). Made me think, "The best of both worlds".

What that means to me now is so much different than what it used to be. The worlds I enjoy living in now are sobriety and happiness. Didn't know that those worlds were one until I met you people and learned the lessons your experiences have taught me. Having fun and living life to its fullest without an unnatural high.

The high I get from simple pleasures of friendship, fellowship and family are the most rewarding.

Love you all.

Riding the turtle,
Phil

September 30, 2011

Good Morning,

I have a speech outline due and I have procrastinated for too long. I will get it done. But now I feel the pressure of it being due. Which made me think I did the same thing in my life and I feel the pressure of all that procrastination like I have to be in a hurry for the test is just around the corner.

The thing is there is no final in life. The whole thing is a class. The test comes after the class. This is the time for studying and part of the lesson is living. I would not be ready for the next part of the lesson without having learned all that I have already.

The hardships I have been through have tendered me in some ways and hardened me in others. All of that so I could be where I am right now, right here, but most importantly, right for the next lesson. So when I look back I have to remember all of that has led me to here, and here is pretty dang good.

Love you all,

Riding the turtle,
Phil

October 2011

October 1, 2011

I really do dislike the days when I feel sorry for myself. It would be so nice if I didn't have those at all. But those are the days that I learn, if I just don't use, if I just don't pick up, it will all be alright. Yesterday a whole bunch of little things all piled up and the load felt intolerable. It wasn't and today I am ok and past those things. I also learned that when I start letting just a few of my responsibilities slip I am heading down the wrong path.

Today my kids come first, tomorrow the house comes first. So we are off to go play. Tomorrow is a day of responsibility to the house and to my school. So Monday I can go recharge without worry of what yet has to be done. Some turtles are harder to ride than others. But I am climbing back on.

October 2, 2011

Good Morning,
Last night a friend was going thru a hard time. The disease was banging on their door. What occurred to me was, it's easy to stay clean when all is well. When life is going good and the monster is locked away. The measure of your program comes when the monster is in your face. When I am at my lowest is when I have to fight my hardest. This thing always shows up at the worst times. When that time comes, if I am not ready, I will lose the fight. But if I am ready the monster never shows. Every time I was not ready, my friends were ready and available to help or I sat myself down and hung on with everything I had till it passed. When I survive those worst times clean, I have that strength available for the next battle. I like waking up guilt free of yesterday.

Love you all,
Phil

October 3, 2011

Good Morning,
Dad came in town yesterday, He is an inspiration in many ways. His attitude seems to almost always be positive. He is always the first one to jump into any chore. His energy seems almost as boundless as his enthusiasm. His support for myself and all my friends warms my heart and the hearts of all who know him. He speaks constantly of how impressed he is with program and the people he meets that are involved in it. He jokes that he is thinking about trying addiction just so he can get some of the recovery he sees us sharing. That speaks volumes about this program and the people in it. I have to say I agree.

Love you

Phil Krause

October 4, 2011

Good Morning,
Yesterday was such a good time. The fellowship and fun was a wonderful way to recharge the soul. I remember when I first got here how confused I felt, what will I do for fun now? The experiences I have had since I have met you all answered that question with ease.

To feel the joy in my heart as a group of past "feeling numbing junkies" laughed and smiled, shit some even skipped (even saw one hula dance) with joy and they were all sober. I don't think that being sober was the thing that did it though. It was the recovery in their lives that made room for the joy to move in, the desire to live better lives as better human beings. Happy, joyous and free. Thanks to all who made that day so special. Those who went and those who didn't

Love you all,
Phil

Thanks again Pops. You did a wonderful and generous thing yesterday. People including me will carry the joy of yesterday in their hearts for a long time. You are one special man. Love ya. Hope last night was fun and you enjoyed your show.

October 5, 2011

Good Morning,
Late to bed and early to rise is not what works best for this guy. My routine has varied some lately. I need to focus. I have been slacking and distracted, time to realign my priorities or give myself a little bit of a break. ... that is the question of the day. I am carrying 16 hours at school. I have been making Straight A's but have not been making as many meetings and am beginning to feel a little burned out. So do I suck it up and keep on keeping on or do I drop a class and ease up on myself. This is a decision I have to make. I get to make this decision with a clear head. That is the most important part. Not something I am used to being able to do. Time to do a little soul searching. I am grateful for the clarity of mind and glad for these problems and not others.

Love you al,
Riding the turtle,
Phil

October 6, 2011

Good Morning,
Yesterday and last night one of the blessings of following the program was made very apparent to me. I had three people share with me the most precious of gifts (get your minds out of the gutter, not that), trust. They shared with me things they want no one else to know. At first it wasn't obvious to me what a gift they had given me. As the day wore on it dawned on me just how much faith they were putting in me and how lucky I was to have someone believe in me that much. Was a reminder that I need to have faith in myself as well as God and my true friends in the program. I love you all dearly.

Ride the turtle,
Phil

Here is one that came in after my morning text that touched me a lot.

You seemed pretty positive already. Just a quick word to say how grateful I am for your friendship. I know you have a lot on your plate and you seem to take it all so easily. That is why people flock to you. You truly have been blessed. Love you man.

A Glimpse of the Journey

October 7, 2011

Good Morning,

I have been watching some friends of mine struggle to experience clean time. The fight is exhausting to them. A constant battle of wants. For the first couple of months I remember fighting that fight. Then my head cleared and I began to understand there was more out there than just being clean. I saw peace and joy in people and I wanted what they had. The problem with that is I couldn't see what they really had. Because I couldn't imagine it. To experience recovery you have to be patient. That's what made it hard for me. I was not a patient man. I wish I could show them the joys that come with recovery. Then the fight would be easy. The reward is not the process. The process is the work. The reward is the freedom that comes from experiencing the process.

Ride the turtle,
Phil

October 8, 2011

Good Morning,
I went to a meeting last night and the topic was "just for today". It occurred to me while people were sharing that living just for today is like holding a watermelon seed between my fingers. I can do it if I let it rest on my finger just letting it happen. But just as soon as I get scared or feel uncomfortable like I might drop it and apply pressure it flies from between my fingers racing into the regrets about the past or racing forward into worry about the future. If I can just resist squeezing for what I want, all will be well. The further I go along in the program the easier it is to just hold still and wait. Like surrendering to win was a concept I couldn't understand so was "just for today".

Love you all,
Ride the turtle,
Phil

A Glimpse of the Journey

October 9, 2011

Good Morning,
Last night family and friends went to the Haunted House down in Branson. It was a lot of fun. One of my friends was quite scared by an actor with a chainsaw. He would start up a chainsaw right as you came around a corner and chase you with it. When we were through we talked about the experience and I told them that the saw had no chain on it and they were slightly embarrassed. This morning it made me think about my fears, how many of the things I have run away from. How many chainless chainsaws I had wasted energy on. Running away from something because I was afraid. Afraid of failure or success, feelings, relationships, school, etc. The program gives me insight and the strength to face those fears. So today I will face my fears and work on my steps.

Love you all,
Phil

October 10, 2011

Good Morning,
Growth is sometimes an ebb and flow. I had some drama in my life yesterday. After it was over I was a bit down. I had reacted not as well as I could have and was feeling bad about it. Then it was pointed out to me that my reaction although not perfect was a vast improvement from the way I would have reacted just a few short months ago. That realization helped me to refocus and understand how much this life of mine is improving. The day to day improvement is hard to see. When I look at the big picture I can see how far I have come. That makes the struggle worth while.

Love you all,
Ride the turtle,
Phil

October 11, 2011

Good Morning,
It dawned on me that some of the things I think I want are probably not coming because I have other things that need to be accomplished first. I have been searching for the wrong things. Chasing physical instead of spiritual. Chasing experiences instead of knowledge. When the knowledge will bring the experiences. Focus Phil, Focus.

Love you all,
Ride the turtle,
Phil

Double dose of Good Morning,
A shorter way of saying the same thing, "Damn I have been looking for the answers when I don't even know what the questions are."

Love you all,
Phew but that turtle was tall:
Phil

Phil Krause

October 12, 2011

Good Morning,
I sometimes struggle with staying the course. Getting my head in the right place was a fight. But once I was there it seemed easy to maintain. Yeah right. I always forget about the constant vigilance part. I get caught up in the day to day activities of life and all of a sudden my head is veering off onto the wrong road. Until I get a firm grip on this new direction in life I have to watch the road closely and focus on where I am now in order to get where I have to be. I have a lot coming up this week: divorce court dates, homework assignments, and a trip up to the lake to help Dad, etc.

Stay clean, stay focused is all I need to know right now. The rest will come. Thank you all for letting me share this way. You have no idea how much it helps.

Love you all,
Ride the turtle,
Phil

A Glimpse of the Journey

October 13, 2011

Good Morning,
Today's reading is a bit ironic to me. One year ago today people all over were reading about how today they would perform one act of kindness. One year ago today was the day that changed my life. The worst thing I ever did to someone else is also the best thing that could have happened to me. One year ago today I realized that the life I was living could not go on. This is not my clean date, but the day that started this process for me. However my past is behind me and future now is brighter than it ever was before. Today my act of kindness is to forgive myself for that and move on. I could not have come this far without all of you and this program. For you and for that I am grateful. So thank you family. Today I am free of yesterday and hopeful for tomorrow.

Love you all,
Riding the turtle,
Phil

October 14, 2011

Good Morning,
Yesterday afternoon I spent some time with a friend. We walked in the park and talked, went for a stroll. Been a long time since I strolled. Later that evening with another friend the three of us and my kids hung out at the house, ordered pizza and laughed and joked. During the time we all spent together I slowed down and relaxed. The importance of taking the time to smell the flowers really hit home. How wonderful life is when I take the time to stroll through it, seeing all there is to see. When I rush through I miss the little things. Addiction rushed me through way too much of my life missing way too many of the little joys never seeing the small precious flowers God has put in my life. Never Again. Never Alone took on new meaning.

Love you all,
Ride the turtle,
Phil

October 16, 2001

Good Morning,
Over the weekend I was having a talk with one of my son's friends. He is facing a few challenges. I shared with him that anyone can get into trouble and get bad grades, anyone can go out and do things the wrong way. I did it and most people I know have done it. But there are a few, a small select group of my peers who have been successful in life. Those people who have stayed the course, who have made more good decisions than bad ones and are the people who impress me the most. That by staying on track now in his life, he can sway the balance of power and end up as one of those select few. Then I realized it could, from now on, be myself who joined the ranks of the successful. It's never too late to lead a better life. If I just make good decisions.

Love you all,
Phil

October 17, 2011

Good Morning,
Last night (after being railroaded) I was sitting in my chair thinking about the job at hand. Feeling the weight of a new responsibility, then my thoughts turned to trust. This responsibility that I have been asked to perform requires others have a lot of trust in me. Me this recovering addict the same guy who took advantage of others, the same guy who used money as "green paper, that when I got rid of it, it turned into a good time." Amazing. So I still have to give some thought to accepting this responsibility. But the act of trusting me has given me renewed faith, in this program, in myself and in God. Thanks to that small group of people for asking… Well not asking, but…. Telling me they trust me.

Ride the turtle,
Love you all,
Phil

A Glimpse of the Journey

October 18, 2011

Good Morning,
When I first came into the rooms sharing my pain with others made my life bearable. To be able to have an ear that would listen eased my pain. I appreciated that so much. It took some time, time spent listening to others to realize that what I was sharing was doing just as much for the people in the rooms as it was me. The compassion I have learned for others is such a huge part of my life. I listen as others share where they are and my heart pours out to them. I would have thought it would empty out. But it doesn't. It becomes more full. I believe that I am just beginning to understand "we only keep what we have by giving it away." Thank you all for being my friends, my guides and my charges.

I love you all,
Riding the turtle,
Phil

October 19, 2011

Good Morning,
The harder I try to grip something the less of it I have. That has happened time and again. My marriage slipped between my fingers, and my faith while in my addiction did the same. I seem to forget that if I relax and let life happen around me that life happens anyway and always turns out for the best. Seems when I grasp for the golden ring of my future I only tarnish its beauty. But if I ride the merry go round and enjoy the view, the ring falls into my lap. My responsibility is to get on and stay on the ride. Do the footwork and let the rest happen. Faith can be renewed by a simple knock on the wall delivered by Angels sent from a friend. You just have to listen for the knock and understand what it means.

Love you all,
Ride the turtle,
Phil

A Glimpse of the Journey

October 20, 2011

Good Morning,

Being cautious was never one of my strong suits. I was always the first to dive right in. I enjoy the thrill of jumping headlong into the unknown. Not knowing what the results would be and figuring I would deal with the consequences when they came along. Sometimes that worked out well, sometimes not so well. I never planned anything. To tell the truth I don't really know how. The only thing I planned on was having a good time. I don't know that the planning part of my life has changed all that much. I still enjoy being impulsive. Going and doing at the drop of a hat is exciting. The big difference now is that I can remember doing it and know that at least my head was clear when I decided to do it and I am willing to accept the consequences. Think I will keep that up. Because now the consequences are mostly rewards.

Ride the turtle,
Phil

October 21, 2011

Good Morning,
This copied from another Daily meditation that I read every morning. It struck me pretty hard.

It is ingrained in us that we have to do exceptional things for God???? but we do not.
We have to be exceptional in the ordinary things of life, and holy on the ordinary sstreets, among ordinary people???and this is not learned in five minutes.

Funny how it can be such work to be average in the ordinary things in life, let alone exceptional. Today I have a year clean. Today I see the light at the end of a tunnel. Not a tunnel I wanted to walk through, but all the chapters in life must end. Not happy it's over, but not sad either. Excited about what the future holds. Learning to have hope was not learned in five minutes either. I found that hope with your help. Think I will stick around.

So goodbye to the old and hello to what ever the future holds!

Love you all,
Ride the turtle,
Phil

A Glimpse of the Journey

October 22, 2011

Good Morning,

I remember the fear of quitting being overwhelming. Worrying that the pain would be too great, dreading the aches and the uncontrollable emotions. The fear of the unknown, how would I act? How could I make it through the day? But as it turns out, it was like everything else. I made it worse in my head than it truly was. Seems that is still one of the things I must learn to handle differently. I finally signed my divorce paperwork yesterday. The feeling of being free from the uncertainty. What a relief. Closing that door and looking forward to the adventure of finding the one that opens is exciting. It has been a rough road but it is behind me and I am stronger for it and free to pursue a better life. A new adventure awaits.

Love you all,
Ride the turtle,
Phil

October 23, 2011

Good Morning,
A friend of mine and myself often joke that we feel like puppets on a string. That very often the subjects that are spoken about in the rooms follow a trend. The trend lately seems to have been forgiveness. I struggle with that myself, some days I have no resentments, or they are not obvious to me. The day will pass by with only good thoughts and my eyes become adjusted to the light of being happy, joyous and free. Then all of a sudden the blackness of my anger overwhelms me and I stumble around in the dark of my past. thinking about how I was wronged and plotting revenge. That is when I hit my knees and pray for the light again, call my friends and talk about spiritual principles. I know that without letting go of that past there is no future.

Ride the turtle,
Phil

A Glimpse of the Journey

October 24, 2011

Good Morning,

Yesterday I spoke with another addict and found that our paths had crossed before. In their addiction some of their actions created a job opportunity for me which allowed me not to have to ….Long story short, she stole, I guarded. Now we didn't know we were helping each other, but we were. Now in this life I can help again, not just that person, but all of the people who want what I have and they don't have to steal it. I am giving it away. I like this reciprocal relationship better. Carrying the message is the greatest gift I can give another. Living the message is the greatest gift I can give myself and everyone around me.

Love you all,
Ride the turtle,
Phul

October 25, 2011

Good Morning,
It was pointed out to me that I signed my text yesterday, "Phul". Okay, a simple mistake, however the chosen pronunciation is to be argued. The "pointer outer" said that it was pronounced "fool". I prefer to think it should be pronounced "full". Full of relationships that do not have boundaries set by greed or dishonesty Full of friendships that are true and know no conditions. Full of gratitude for all my friends that are true and know no conditions. Full of gratitude for all my friends and family who have supported me through the difficult times and seen me through to the place I am now. Full of love even for the fools who have pronunciation problems. Ok, ok so it's a gratitude text with a small jab thrown in.

Love you all,
Ride the turtle,
Phil

October 26, 2011

Good Morning,
The definition of forgiveness is to give up the right to punish. This can be hard to do when you feel hurt, when the pain is not just your own but effects the ones you love. The best way I have found to get relief is to pray. Seems every time I pray the anger subsides. The right to punish fades a little more. Time heals all wounds. I have to remember who's time that happens in. If I am honest, open-minded and willing, it will happen. So friends today please throw a prayer in for those who need forgiveness and for those who need to forgive. I am both of those people, so are we all.

Love you all,
Ride the turtle,
Phil

October 27, 2001

Good Morning,
Last night I was talking to a fellow addict about how much I enjoy this new life, how much I appreciate people now, how much I appreciate people's compassion for one another. It used to be that if it didn't benefit me I didn't care. Yesterday I watched this friend from a distance taking time out of her day to talk to a senior citizen. My friend was tired and worn out, wanted nothing more than to get some rest. But she stopped and smiled and talked. Forgetting about herself and her problems for just a moment just to spend a moment with someone who needed just to be recognized. Warmed my heart and touched my soul. Reminded me to slow down, share my time. If not for me or that person, maybe for someone else I don't know who is watching.

Love you all,
Ride the turtle,
Phil

A Glimpse of the Journey

October 28, 2011

Good Morning,
Yesterday I was driving with Bailey and a friend and I was amazed at the fall colors, the changing of the leaves is beautiful. I started to think about how I couldn't remember the last time we had so much color. It seemed it had been years since the last time the colors had been so brilliant and vibrant. I wondered what could be making such a change this year. Why was everything so much more colorful? Then it dawned on me that this was the first time in years that I had looked. I can only see how wonderful things are around when I look for the wonderful things. If I spend my time looking for the bad, that is all I will see. If I spend my time looking for the beauty, that is what I will see. Today I think I will look for the good.

Love you all,
Ride the turtle,
Phil

Phil Krause

October 29, 2011

Good Morning,

Yesterday I was in a meeting and a person that I respect very much was there, someone who when they share I always gain knowledge from. As always the words they spoke were very insightful and meaningful to me. I listened to those who shared and when it was my turn I stumbled through what came to mind and passed. The meeting finished. I gathered my things and got ready to go. As I said my goodbyes this person came to me and told me that they always enjoyed hearing what I had to say. WHAT? Who were they talking to? To think that someone so grounded in their recovery could sift through what I thought and find some nugget of meaning in that. The point being, that we all contribute to each other's recovery. Thank you all for being there for me and my recovery.

Love you all,

Phil

A Glimpse of the Journey

October 30, 2011

Good Morning,
I had a wonderful time last night. I enjoyed the company of friends and fellowship. It's amazing to me to watch such a diverse group of people get together and have such a fun time. This new life is amazing and to share it with all of you is a blessing. Hard to believe I was scared of this life, not knowing that there could be this much joy, this much beauty, this much freedom and this much fun. I haven't felt this way since I was a kid. Wish my kids could have been there. They would have had a great time.

Love you all,
Ride the turtle,
Phil

October 31, 2011

Good Morning,
I keep feeling milestones in my recovery, little rewards for changing the way I view things. The ability to stay centered for longer periods of time and through times of stress and hardship. To be able to look back on a disagreement and be proud of the way I handled myself, to not be building a regret for tomorrow. To talk to someone who seems miles away in belief or attitude and see that common ground. To be able to look at a situation and be ok with it, to not have to impose my ideas and my will on someone else, to not have to make that suggestion of how "I would do that" just to make myself feel important, to care enough for someone else to not help, to step back and do what's best for everyone else but me. That's a tough one, but very rewarding.

Love you all,
Phil

November 2011

November 2, 2011

Good Morning,
I have been feeling a little under the weather lately and yesterday I decided to take the morning and rest as opposed to going to a meeting. Big mistake. I ended up having an argument with the kids' mom. Still not quite sure what started the whole thing, but that didn't matter. She jigged the rope and I picked up my end. Away we went. I know better. I have done very well over the past few months at just not participating in her silly drama. I don't have to put on my clown suit just because she does. I don't have to act out just because she wants me to. So today I prayed for her to find peace in her heart, for her to be able to live a life without all that anger, to find the joy that I have found. Please pray for her. For all our sakes.
Thanks,
Love you all,
Phil

November 3, 2011

Good Morning,
One of the signs I have to watch for is when I start vilifying myself and others. When I start to think about what a bad person I am and how I have to start showing other people what a tough guy I am, I am letting the negative take over again. That's when I need to stop and make some phone calls, stop plotting my revenge and start plotting my recovery. I have to work the fields of my program, go back and look at where I am, why I am here and what has gotten me to this far. I can be a vengeful, spiteful asshole. But that is not what gives me a happy tomorrow. It is so easy for me to revert back. But is so healthy for me to not. So today I will not take the old familiar paths. I will reap what I have sown over the past year.

Love you all,
Ride the turtle,
Phil

A Glimpse of the Journey

November 4, 2011

Good Morning,

Like puppets on a string, many times it seems there is a common theme that runs through the rooms or through our lives. Having gone through the relationship issues I have has left me insecure and damaged, afraid to open my heart all the way, cautious about sharing my love with others. This morning's meditation speaks of exchanging love, giving and receiving. This exchange has to be equal. It has to be balanced. I worry that I may not be capable of giving of myself freely, or of feeling "short changed" because I give too much. The relationships I have had in the past I thought were healthy when they were good and when I was in them. Now I wonder if I know what a healthy relationship is and if I am capable of having one. Time to get my ass back into my steps.

Love you all,
Ride the turtle,
Phil

November 5, 2011

Good Morning,
Sorry about the delay in the morning text. I was being of service this morning, which reminded me of the importance of family. What a big part of our lives my family is, the ones I am blood with and my NA family. Going to keep this short this morning. Just want you all to know how much you mean to me.

Love you all,
Ride the turtle,
Phil

A Glimpse of the Journey

November 6, 2011

Good Morning,
Yesterday evening I spent a little time with some people I barely know. They live in the country and are good people with old-fashioned ideas and morals. They know a friend of mine who is in the program and our conversation turned to recovery and the roads that led me down this path. Even after sharing some of my past and telling them about the man I was, they asked me to come back. They offered me a place to hunt and when I left told me how nice it was to have spent time together. It wasn't very long ago that these same kind of people would have shunned me and made it clear that I wasn't welcome back. The only promise is freedom from active addiction. The truth is that promise only scratches the surface of the blessings that may come a person's way.

Love you all,
Turtle Phil

November 7, 2011

Letting things happen can be such a challenge. I would never have thought that doing nothing could be so hard and yet so rewarding. Lately I have seen so many wonderful things happen, time to spend with friends where there was no time available, introductions to people I never would have thought I would get to meet, a new friend where I thought there was a distance. Freedoms that seemed forever away have suddenly arrived without warning. None of those things would have happened ….Or at least none would have happened without guilt or shame had I stuck my grimy little fingers in the works. Listening to and watching "the hows" to live has paid off beyond my wildest dreams. Somehow I have learned to just relax, it's going to be alright.

Love you all,
Ride the turtle,
Phil

A Glimpse of the Journey

November 8, 2011

Good Morning,
I was reading the daily meditation and thinking of how insane my life used to be. One of the things I fight with is keeping the insanity out of my life. I am forced almost daily to deal with insanity, the freedom for me does not apply to all those around me. There are people in and out of the program that are stuck in that "insanity rut". Forced exposure to these people is one of the things I am powerless over. However I do not have to participate in the insanity. Oh but sometimes I want to. Sometimes my better judgment flies out the window like money out of my pocket during my addiction. However if I pause, reflect where that action will take me, I can usually keep the insanity at bay. So the "key" for me is the pause.

Love you all,
Ride the turtle,
Phil

November 9, 2011

Good Morning,
Some of you know that I am a wood worker. Several years back I met a man who is also a wood worker and we struck up a friendship. He built the most amazing pieces of furniture. One of these pieces was a highboy dresser, very elaborate with hidden compartments etc, at about the same time I built a bed. I was visiting him and was admiring his work and he began to point out flaws. Things I never would have seen. He picked the piece apart. Later he was checking out the bed I had built and went on about how much he liked it. I was shocked because the bed I had made was full of flaws that he would have never seen except I pointed them out. The point, we build the bed of our lives. We make all the mistakes or flaws and know they are there. Everyone else sees the most amazing human.

Love you all,
Ride the turtle,
Phil

A Glimpse of the Journey

November 10, 2011

Good Morning,

I have had some harsh discussions with my ex over the last few weeks. It has been frustrating and time consuming. Fighting with her has left me on edge. I said to a friend how difficult she can be to deal with. Is it that she is difficult to deal with? Or is it that I allow her to be difficult to deal with? Last night for the first time in a long time she was nice to me, said "thank you" and "you're welcome" and some other very confusing words. I am so prepared to jump when I deal with her that I was almost as mad at her for being nice as I would have been if she were to have been rude. So is it her or is it me that makes me mad? No matter how someone else acts I am the only person who controls how I feel. Today I will remember that.

Love you all,
Ride the turtle,
Phil

November 12, 2011

Good Morning,
Going through what we have to go through can be so difficult when we are doing everything right. I remember coming into the program hoping that it would save my marriage. The pain that I suffered as I watched that fall apart was not relieved by staying sober. The marriage still failed. But I was ok and I was clean. The program helped me though, as long as I didn't use, my head stayed clear I was open to suggestions from the program. As long as I stayed open, I gained some recovery and some perspective. I am willing to do what it takes to continue my recovery. Go through what I have to go through as long as I do it clean, all will be ok.

Love you all,
Ride the turtle,
Phil

A Glimpse of the Journey

November 13, 2011

Good Morning,
I read two daily meditations every morning. NA's today speaks of progress not perfection, the other speaks of being perfectly attuned to Jesus, to not have any fears. I believe that fear is healthy and human. I also believe courage is healthier. To be afraid but to have the courage to face those fears builds our courage. I was afraid of what my life would be like in recovery only to find out that I should have been afraid of living without recovery. I was afraid I couldn't be a good father to my children, only to find that I am and can always be. I could have run, I would never have learned the joys of being a good single parent. Today I have fear, but I also have courage and so do all of you. Another reason I am proud to call you friends.

Love you all,
Ride the turtle,
Phil

November 14, 2011

Good Morning,

Trust is something I have always had a problem with. Sometimes I gave it too freely when I should not have and sometimes I was too conservative when I should have been generous. Finding that balance is difficult. Today I give out just a little bit to someone and wait. If all goes well I give a little more. I did the same thing with the program. I started not wanting to trust at all. Slowly as I learned a few of the principles I trusted more. I was not being asked to give up anything (I had decided to try to give up drugs) but could gain a lot. I saw others trust in the program and the rewards were great. More than anything else I learned to trust myself just being trustworthy. I learned to follow that spiritual voice inside that told me to do the right thing.
Love you all,
Phil

November 15, 2011

Good Morning,

I have been fighting some obsessive thoughts again lately, not "using" thoughts but obsessive thought just the same. Usually to do with my past relationship. I pray about it asking God for knowledge of his will for me, and the power to carry that out, followed by the serenity prayer. Sometimes that works pretty well for me. What seems to work better than that is when I just don't worry about it. I am working on the just not worrying about it. If I occupy my time with schoolwork or meetings or service work it helps. But sometimes I just obsess. I guess that's not a problem as long as I have the time to think about nothing but that. However I just don't have that kind of time. So today I think I will focus on the tasks at hand and worry about getting MY work done, not someone else's.

Love you all,
Ride the turtle,
Phil

November 16, 2011

Good Morning,

I was thinking back on the last year about the situations I was in and the way handled some of the, "I wish I would have…" kind of stuff. The way I might have seen me now if I could have handled it differently. Come to think of it I am pretty happy at the way it all turned out. Trying to be perfect during any time in my life especially those times in my life is insanity. I made it through those times regardless of how anyone including myself thinks of me. To have successfully come through it without using is the miracle. To have made it through at all is a success. I made it through that ok because I didn't use and I didn't die or kill anyone else. Sometimes that is the best I do. Now that I have a handle on the problems of yesterday, I can handle today and work for better results. One thing at a time.

Love you all,
Ride the turtle,
Phil

A Glimpse of the Journey

November 17, 2011

Good Morning,

Every now and again I see the growth. When an event happens that I would have reacted poorly to in the past and I don't react in the old ways I get to see the growth. When I calmly face what would have been an excellent opportunity to throw on the clown suit, I see the growth. That opportunity presented itself yesterday. I calmly assessed the situation, smiled and thought, "no way am I ruining my day and my tomorrow over that". Turn it over to God because it will be what it will be whether I throw a fit or not. The end result will be the same. There is no event that will be made any better by my throwing a fit. There is no situation that will be made any better by me using. So no fits and no using. Seems to work better that way. Think I will keep it up.

Love you all
Phil

November 19, 2011

Good Morning,

To learn from the innocent is a challenge. My children continue to love myself and their mother as we continue down this path of anger and resentment. They are witness to countless conflicts and they continue to love us. They watch me as I get upset with her behavior and they forgive me for being angry at someone they love. I am supposed to be the teacher. As I watch them I am humbled by their ability to love unconditionally. Where do they find the understanding? I am amazed at their resilience. Oh to have the heart of my children. I pray for the desire to have the desire to forgive as they forgive us both endlessly. Today I will learn from my children to have an open and forgiving heart.

Love you all,
Ride the turtle,
Phil

A Glimpse of the Journey

November 20, 2011

Good Morning,

Yesterday I argued with the kids' mother. During our argument she told me it told was easy to be a responsible parent when I was given no choice. That bothered me quite a bit until I realized that I did have a choice. I could have left. I could have run away just like she did. The reason I didn't run away is my love and my devotion to my children. So although I had the option to ditch my responsibility there was no choice. I love my kids too much to put anything about me ahead of them. I have to remember that although I am far from perfect I am a good man who does right by my family and continues to work on making myself as good a man as I can be.

I Love you all,
Ride the turtle,
Phil

Phil Krause

November 20, 2011

Good Morning,

I have to learn to keep my mouth shut. Sometimes I see others behavior and it infuriates me. I have to learn to control that anger so it doesn't affect the people close to me. I have to remember that their behavior can only affect me if I let it. The way I react to it is my testament. The way they behave is theirs. So today I am going to work on not taking and sharing someone else's inventory. Today I will focus on me and my behavior.

Love you all,
Ride the turtle,
Phil

A Glimpse of the Journey

November 21, 2011

Good Morning,

I had a pleasant day yesterday and a relaxing night last night...I got nothing.

Love you all,
Ride the turtle,
Phil

November 22, 2011

Good Morning,

For the last few weeks the morning text has become more and more of a challenge. So I think that's it for now. Going to ease up for a bit.

Love you all,
Ride the turtle,
Phil

November 27, 2011

Good Morning,

Are all expectations wrong? I understand having unrealistic expectations is wrong, but is it unrealistic to expect someone to do what they say they are going to do? I seem to get hurt when I expect people to do what they say they are going to and then they don't do it. I have recently been asked to build something for someone. My shop is where I used to use, a lot. I am not all that comfortable out there. It stirs memories for me. However I did say I would build it. If I don't live up to my word, then I am building resentment from and for me. I have a person in my life that said they would pay me money they owe me and then said they would not. Someone told me resentments are not a luxury we addicts can afford to have. So do I believe nothing people tell me? No choose to have faith in people so they can faith in me.

Love you all,
Ride the turtle,
Phil

November 28, 2011

Good Morning,

I woke up this morning thinking about my weekend feeling pretty good about it. There were some rough spots over the weekend. I had to set some boundaries that resulted in the end of a romantic relationship, but not the end of a friendship. I fought with Ex which resulted in some personal awareness that will bring growth. I spent a lot of my weekend alone but not lonely. Being comfortable alone is a huge step for me. It used to be that I didn't like the company when I was alone. To have had all the ups and downs that I had and to look back and to think that was an ok weekend kind of shocked me. The growth in and of itself can be the positive. How I measure my time doesn't have to the experience. It can be what I learned from it.

Love you all,
Ride the turtle,
Phil

A Glimpse of the Journey

November 29, 2011

Good Morning,

What is that thing that is inside of us that keeps the fire of recovery going? And how do I share that with others? I was at a meeting last night and saw a person I have known for quite some time, out of recovery and in. We started treatment on the same day. In treatment he had a fire inside of him that was inspirational. He now has Four days clean and is returning to the same treatment center we both started. In the past year he has nearly died at least once that I know of. I want recovery for him so much. Powerlessness. Acceptance, humility, compassion……Not much else to say. I love ya Bro and I will be praying for you.

Love you all,
Ride the turtle,
Phil

November 30, 2011

Good Morning,

One of my morning readings reminded me of a young man that went to the same school I went to. He was involved in an accident when he was a boy and lost an arm. His parents encouraged him to do everything that he wanted to do. He had some great excuses to not get involved but instead he involved himself. That young man became a receiver on the football team and started throughout his high school career. He never said "I can't…". He always said "why can't I?" I sometimes wonder what that young man is doing now. I imagine it's something great. I think I will always do my best to remember that young man as I face challenges in my life and ask myself, "why can't I". It doesn't have to be a great thing, as long as it's a good thing, "why can't I".

Love you all,
Ride the turtle,
Phil

December 2011

December 1, 2011

Good Morning,

Turning it all over. Damn but I fight with this one. Cause you know god is awful busy. Maybe he needs just a little help with … I can justify anything. When I do turn it over, everything seems to happen just the way it should, seems to happen better than I ever could imagine. Then it all seems to be going so well, surely I must have had my hand in there somewhere and off to the races we go. Until I have things so messed up I am first stepping again, faith is overcome by forgetfulness, trust overcome by arrogance and hope is lost. But that is what my sponsor, the rooms, and the meetings are for, to remind me of how I got to where I am. My own best thinking. When things are going, I call my sponsor whether things are going good or bad.

Love you all,
Ride the turtle,
Phil

December 2, 2011

Good Morning,

Obsessive thought is one of the toughest things for me to deal with. Seems I get a handle on how to feel about a problem when all of a sudden something that throws my perspective out of kilter is thrown into the mix. My poor little turtle's legs are about wore out running around looking for new perspectives to the same old problem. So I am taking it back to basics.
1. First thought = wrong.
2. Take a minute to think about the problem.
3. Call my sponsor.
4. Bounce some ideas around with people I trust

Then I will make a decision based off of the best information I have at the time. To be forever tied to someone who I don't trust is difficult, especially when I have to trust them with what I love the most.

Love you all,
Ride the turtle,
Phil

A Glimpse of the Journey

December 3, 2011

Good Morning,

The amount of time and energy into the getting finding ways and means it is said that if I put a tenth of that energy into recovery, I would have this thing whipped. Can you imagine if I put a tenth into recovery and another tenth into my life itself? I used to talk about all the things I wanted to do. Now I do the things I talked about wanting to do. I can see a future for myself, a future that includes success, a future that includes happiness, a future for myself, my kids and my loved ones. That hope of a better tomorrow is so much more than I had before, just the hope. The reality of what tomorrow may bring is beyond my imagination. So the hope I have sustains me. The promise of a new future is something I haven't had since I was a child.

Love you all,
Ride the turtle,
Phil

December 4, 2011

Good Morning,

I heard someone speaking of the insanity of addiction yesterday. They spoke with such calmness about insanity that directly affected their lives. My first thought was shock, the oh my god, how can you even think of continued exposure to that kind of life, then it occurred to me that those kinds of activities were not so crazy or unheard of when I lived that lifestyle either. I had a friend who lost a father and two good friends to the violence of addiction in my last year out there and my thoughts were more the "that's a shame" line of thought than of the "my God, that's insane." It takes time and separation to see the truth of the life we lived. It takes time to learn that there is a better life than that one. And it takes time to learn we don't have to live that way.

Phil

A Glimpse of the Journey

December 6, 2011

Good Morning,

I woke to a text that it was white outside. I ran to the door like a child .. not because I had to see that snow, but because my dog had to pee. However, seeing the snow made me think of new beginnings and how happy I am now. Of course I still have frustrations. They are nowhere near as bad as the old ones and I am learning to deal with them better as well. Being given the gift of being able to "hit the reset button" on life is a miracle I did not know was available. Now to be able to reset my mindset whenever I need to saves me from using. As long as I remember that life will continue to get better and not worse, as was the case during my addiction. No having to run and find, no having to get mad because I don't have. Can't believe I lived that way for so long.

Love you all,
Phil

December 7, 2011

Good Morning,

Using the tools I have learned is becoming easier, struggling through the emotions is not. I wrestle with allowing myself to accept and feel the pain when it comes. I know it's natural to feel it. I just don't like to feel it. But I don't have to like it, I just have to do it. Well, I have options. But they are no longer acceptable. I look at my feelings sometimes and wonder why I feel the way I do. I see the relationship between my kids and their Mom improving, which is what I felt I wanted more than anything else. Now as I watch them spending more time with her for some silly reason I feel betrayed. Stupid human emotion. This is not their fault or their feelings to have to deal with. They are mine. Now all I have to do is keep them in check and to the right thing. Embrace the fact that their relationship is improving, that they are getting their Mom back and be happy for them. It is hard though.

Love you all,
Ride the turtle,
Phil

A Glimpse of the Journey

December 8, 2011

Good Morning

A few days ago there was a newcomer brought in by a family member. When this man introduced himself and told of the reason he was in the rooms, that his nephew was heading down the wrong path and he was there to support him the room opened up and the compassion and acceptance flooded the room. I gave this young man my basic text and told him to come back. Yesterday they returned and his uncle approached me, asked if I was an electrician and if I had known a man by the name of Josh Jackson. Josh was a friend of mine who took his own life while in addiction several years ago. His demons caught up with him in the prime of his life. Our lives are so intertwined. Not just this man and my own, all of us. The connection of our commonalities provides compassion. There is nothing I can do for Josh. However, there is something I can do for my fellow man. I can show compassion for we are all connected somehow.

Love you all,
Ride the turtle,
Phil

December 9, 2011

Good Morning,

Choosing the right course of action can really be a challenge, weighing the information, thinking about the options and following through with your decision. Even afterward I still have thoughts and doubts if I have done what is best. The waiting to see the results is hard for me. Patience is a learned spiritual principle that I am working on. The more I wait the more the doubts plague my mind. I have to give life the opportunity to play out without me getting involved again and that is difficult for me. But I will never know if the choices I make are the right ones if I don't give it a chance. The more I wait the more I develop that ability to wait. Very similar to staying clean. Once I have made the decision I have to be willing to give life the chance to improve.

LYA
Phil

A Glimpse of the Journey

December 10, 2011

Good Morning,

The daily meditation speaks about winners and how to identify them. To me that seems easy. Every time I walk into a meeting the room is full of winners or those who are working on it. Every day I stay clean, I win, even if I don't follow all the spiritual principles! EVERY DAY I STAY CLEAN I WIN. I may not have a lot of recovery every day. I make mistakes all the time. If I just don't make the BIG mistake everything will be ok. Everything will work out the way it is supposed to. It's hard for me to remember that sometimes. It keeps happening so I am starting to believe it. Things don't happen in my time. But they do happen and it always works out for the best, somehow. So I keep coming to meetings, working on being a winner. Doing the best I can do.

Love you all,
RTT
Phil

December 11, 2011

Good Morning,

I slept in today, yea. Last night I went to the Christmas party and listened to Red and she was incredible. One of the things she spoke about was self-esteem. I wrestle with this quite a bit. My situation allows me to wonder if I am a good man. I think if I am a good man why would she leave me. I get angry at myself for having these doubts, but don't know how to stop the feelings from running through my head. My friends tell me I am a good Dad. My girlfriend tells me I am a good man. But for some reason I choose to occasionally allow myself to doubt the man I am. I have to assume the true answer is inside me and can be found by working the steps. I will keep gong to meetings, work harder on my step work and look inside myself for my own answers.

Love you all,
Ride the turtle,
Phil

A Glimpse of the Journey

December 12, 2011

Good Morning,

I read a quote this morning that made me stop and think, "It's easier to go down hill than up, but the view is at the top". In my struggle I sometimes forget where I am going. I sometimes forget that at the top of the hill is where I need to be and where my HP wants me to be. If I pause too long looking for directions instead of following the ones I have, gravity takes over and I start to lose ground I have worked so hard to get. Today instead of pausing to look for directions I will follow the ones I have been so generously given. They have gotten countless others to their destination. They will work for me as well.

Love you all,
Ride the turtle,
Phil

December 13, 2011

Good Morning,

Ok, so I am really getting into the quote of the day thing. I like the inspiration of thought it brings. Today's is "Patience is bitter, but its fruit is sweet." Huh, huh, that one is a kicker in the asser, huh? How many times have I denied myself that fruit? As an addict I want things here and now. The whole idea of waiting seemed somehow wrong. Waiting was for other people who couldn't get what they wanted now. Yeah, turns out those other people were smart people who knew that good things, sweet things, rewarding things come to those who wait. Now that I have identified the problem, I will work towards practicing patience. I want to taste the fruit so sweet it satisfies. What does satisfaction taste like? Hope I'm patient enough to find out.

Love you all,
RTT
Phil.

A Glimpse of the Journey

December 14, 2011

Good Morning,

Last night I was in a discussion with a friend about recent events in my life. There were times during the discussion that I was uncomfortable. They were asking me to take a look at the events from a different point of view. I disagreed with their point of view and still do. But the fact that I was uncomfortable made me take a deeper look at the possibility that I was wrong. It used to be that when I was uncomfortable. I would mark that person down as wrong on my list and move on. Today it's ok to be uncomfortable. Differences of opinion are all a part of life. To be able to agree to disagree is ok. That makes that person no less of a friend. It only makes them a friend with different ideas and ideals. It all comes down to acceptance.

Love you all,
Ride the turtle,
Phil

December 15, 2011

Good Morning,

"Nothing leads to good that is not natural." When I read this quote this morning my first thought was of the drugs I put into my body, all the years of putting chemicals into myself. But the more I thought about it, the more I thought about how I feel. I believe we all know at a very young age the difference between right and wrong. That gut feeling that tells you when something is wrong,. The freedom you feel when you are doing something right. It's when I follow those gut feelings and allow my life to happen around me without my interference that my days pass in harmony. The chaos that can exist in life is outside my bubble. The stresses of life minimize and I am free from guilt or shame for that time. I am enjoying settling into this life of harmony.

Love you all,
RTT,
Phil

December 16, 2011

Good Morning,

Yesterday was spent with friends hunting pirates' gold. We found no gold, but plenty of treasure. The people I spend time with are a direct reflection of who I am. The people I choose to runaround with have traits I admire. They teach me things, like how to laugh when I'm down, compassion when I am up, how to live not just exist. They teach me how to walk through the hard times and live with some sense of dignity and decency. It can be hard sometimes for when I care so much about other people share their struggles. I feel the pain as they walk thought difficult times. But it also lightens my load when they share mine with me. I am so grateful to have you all as my friends to help carry your loads and to have the help carrying mine.

Love you all,
Ride the turtle,
Phil

December 17, 2011

Good Morning,

There are places I really should not go, no not like drug bad places, but physical places that are not good for me emotionally. When I go there it has a negative effect on me. So I do my best to stay away. I hate the feeling of being limited on the where I can go. I pray and I do my best to disassociate myself. Even when I am successful, I don't feel good about the way I feel when I leave. Sorry this is all so vague but I have no choice. The point is I don't like having lack of control over my emotions. I would very much so like to be able to go where I want or where I need to go without fear of emotional pain. Some places are just forever linked to emotions, some happy some not so happy. Damn these silly human emotions. Thank god for all of you.

Love you all,
RTT
Phil

A Glimpse of the Journey

December 20, 2011

Good Morning,

Though I relish our warm months, winter is when character is made and our best comes out. Through the toughest of times is when we get to find out what metal we are made of. Are we weak and give in to the easy path? Those roads we have walked so many times in the past, or do we strive to improve ourselves by digging deep and finding out just what we are capable of enduring. My children inspire me to keep digging. I was given the blessing of watching my little girl go to school yesterday knowing she was not feeling well, knowing her heart was broken, but knowing she had finals and a job to do. I like to think that some of that came from me. My children watched as I went to school when I was not feeling well. They watched as I did my job with a broken heart.

Love you all,
Phil

December 21, 2011

Good Morning,

"Supreme excellence consists in breaking the enemy's resistance without fighting." This is a quote from Sun Tzu and the art of war. Sounds an awful lot like part of our twelve traditions and something I need to remember and work on. Attraction not promotion. I rarely promote, but how often do I attract? Are my actions of the attracting kind? I am getting better at that. But there is always room for improvement. In my case, a lot of room. Just as my using affected all those around me, so does, or so should my recovery. To not fight to win is still something I struggle with. The line between passivity and doormat sometimes gets fuzzy. I practice on that quite a bit. I think I shall practice that more today than I did yesterday.

Love you all,
RTT
Phil

A Glimpse of the Journey

December 22, 2011

Good Morning,

I think back on how chaotic my life was before and how simple my life can be now. There are times of peace and they are directly connected to my behavior. When I relax, enjoy the simple things, my life follows that same path. When I start to clutter my world with negative thought, thoughts of what my life should be or how it could be, I feel the chaos closing in. When I live my life as it is, I feel content and at ease. I don't know why I fall into moments of self-sabotage. Old habits I assume and they are difficult to let go of all the time. I am however improving. The moments of peace get longer and the moments of chaos get further apart. When I focus on the moment I get to enjoy it more.

Love you all,
RTT
Phil

December 23, 2011

Good Morning,

"Great thoughts speak only to the thoughtful mind, but great actions speak to all mankind." When I read this I thought the rooms is where we learn the actions that we carry with us to the outside. The first action I learned was just don't use. Once I learn that, the rest comes as it comes. How fast it comes is up to me. If I want to act differently faster, I go to a lot of meetings, work the steps and be of service. Most importantly I learn not to use. Then I learn how to live while I don't use. That's the part I am working on, making mistakes along the way is ok, hard to accept, but ok. I get frustrated sometimes, but that's ok too. I am learning, defining the new me.

Love you all,
RTT
Phil

December 26, 2011

Good Evening

I just got home from visiting with family and have missed my connection with all of you. Over the holiday I struggled with my emotions and faced some hard emotional times. My thoughts turned to loyalty and how difficult it can be to find. There are only a few people that I trust completely, only a few that I know I can count on. Those people are my inner circle and my first line of defense when I fall on hard times. Those people have proven themselves time and time again, even with that I know I have to have more to lean on so I pray. I pray a lot. Those prayers carry me through until my inner circle answers the phone or shows up at my door. Most people in life are variables. There are few constants. When I find one they have my loyalty. Thank you my loyal friends.

Love you all,
RTT
Phil

December 27, 2011

Good Morning,

In my early recovery and even some now, I spent a lot of my time wondering what might have been. I kicked myself for my behavior and wished I would have done this or that. I wondered what my life would have been like if I had taken a different path. Now more often than not I wonder what my life will be like, where am I going and what can I turn this life into. Now I make the choices. I am not forced into a life of confusion, but a life of possibilities, a life of clarity and peace, as long as I choose to not react to the past or the negative, but to the now and the positive. Life has thrown me some curve balls and I have walked back to the bench many times. This is not bottom of the ninth, but top of the fourth.

Love you all,
Ride the turtle,
Phil

A Glimpse of the Journey

December 28, 2011

Good Morning,

My actions and my behaviors have landed me in the spot I am in. There are things about this spot that I love and things about this spot that I am not pleased about. This is however my spot whether I choose to decorate it with happiness or sadness is up to me. I fight with letting go of the gloom and doom some days and others my spot is painted manly car yellow. The happiness I seek, when found outside of me, is fleeting. I have to look in to find sustained happiness. That happiness can be elusive, hiding behind my fears and ducking in and out of the shadows of my regrets. When I find my happiness, it seems to always be in the right now. The hard part is when I don't see it and go looking in my past or worry about the future. I am happy about who I am right now.

Love you all,
Phil

December 29, 2011

Good Morning,

Quote of the day, "nothing is easy to the unwilling." That, I think is the biggest answer to this program. When I left the old world behind I was more than willing and I still am. I had tried to get clean many times before with little to no success. When I was forced to take a look at that man I had become and didn't like what I saw, was when I became willing. All the times before I was so tired I couldn't get out of bed. I would lay in bed and sleep for weeks on end, feeling dope sick and seeing no relief in sight until I gave in. This time I couldn't lay there. There were things to do that meant the difference between whether I wanted to live or die. I had to find something worth living for and I found that in the rooms, that life I had been missing.

Love you all,
RTT
Phil

December 30, 2011

Good Morning,

I have been thinking a lot lately about the friends I have and the friends I used to have. I used to have many friends but very little friendship. The people I ran around with spent as much time screwing me over as I did them and we called ourselves friends. The friends I have now spend time expressing their friendship as I do the same for them, making ourselves available to one another for the important things in life. I used to think that a dope run or a front was an expression of friendship. The friends I have now and the way they express their friendship is in no way the same as the people I thought were friends from before. I thank God I now have friends. I am thanking God for all of you.

Love you all,
RTT
Phil

January 2012

January 1, 2012

Good Morning,

The meditation today talks about vigilance, remaining watchful for trouble, being aware of our behavior and the signs we are falling back on old behavior. When we do revert to our old ways spotting those things and implementing change. Setting boundaries and enforcing those boundaries can be a challenge as well. As soon as I drop my guard, open my mind, just a little bit of old behavior creeps back in and my addiction is ready and waiting. I have no room in my life for the drama or the heartache it brings along with it. My addiction acts like it cares about me. It wants me to believe it is good for me and wants the best for me. I sometimes start to believe it. But I have been lucky enough to see the lies early enough to avoid falling for the trap. I must remain vigilant or die.

Love to all,
RTT
Phil

A Glimpse of the Journey

January 2, 2012

Good Evening,

Today I am keeping my mind open. I sometimes revert back to old thinking and close my head. I must remain teachable. I used to say that the one electrician I never want to work with is the one who says he knows it all. That person will get you killed. It's much the same in NA. The person who goes to meetings just to speak scares me. I seek counsel from people who are more experienced than I, have lived through the things I am facing, especially the ones who made it through but suffered consequences for their actions for those are the people with experience. They know what doesn't work. There is a lot to learn from someone who knows what doesn't work. I learn the most at meetings where I don't expect it and I am glad I remain teachable.

Love you all,
RTT
Phil

January 3, 2012

Good Morning,

I have heard it said that a person should be judged by their questions not by their answers. Who am I now? Not what was I before? Where am I going" Not where have I been? I like to think that I was a pretty nice guy before, but prefer to be a nice guy now. My past keeps biting me in the butt, especially when I try to include the people from my past. When I focus on the now and the people in my life now, life seems to flow along smoothly. When I concentrate on the things I have to do today, I accomplish those things and my today goes along smooth. Worry about yesterday and tomorrow takes up a lot of time from the things I have to do today. Today I will focus on today.

Love you all,
RTT
Phil

January 4, 2012

Good Morning,

When I read the morning meditation it spoke of being free of the guilt and shame of my addiction, being free of the obsession to use has not freed me from guilt and shame. It has given me the ability to not create anymore if I choose to not create anymore. Not doing the next right thing is where that guilt and shame comes from. The days when I am just clean are the days I usually create more. The days when I am doing the next right thing are the days when I don't have room in my life to create more. The days I focus on what Phil has to do today, just that. Not what can Phil do today, not how can Phil do things today. Just doing the things I have to do. When those things are done is the time I get to do other things, healthy things.

Love you all,
RTT
Phil

Phil Krause

January 6, 2012

Good Afternoon,

Patience is a skill I work on daily. I have never been a good waiter. I find myself growing frustrated and my mind goes to work roaming around in areas that are not healthy for me. This program and the relationships I have developed in it help me to recognize this defect and allow me to evaluate my feelings and focus on the solutions instead of the problem. So today I practice developing the skill of patience, improving myself and finding ways to be a better waiter.

Love to all,
RTT
Phil

A Glimpse of the Journey

January 7, 2012

Good Morning,

In the past several months I have become more and more content with who I am and where I am in my life. I was also told that I am a diamond in the rough and when I complete my steps there will be a light in my life and in my character that I will have never known. I have been hung u on my 4th step for quite some time now and don't feel as though it is from fear but from contentment. However, there is no way to find out if what I have been told is true unless I plunge in and complete my stepwork. I go back to school on the 17th of January and have made someone a promise that I will complete 4 and 5 by that time. I have been satisfied with content before in my life, time to try something new and see where this leads me. So today I will set aside time for stepwork.

Love you all

January 9, 2012

Good Morning,

This is a variation on a quote I read this morning, "going to NA and not getting involved is like having a wrapped present and not opening it". Getting involved in NA is what made the difference for me. When you get involved by going to meetings and sharing your struggles is how people get to know the real you. They hear the things that make you familiar to them. The commonalities that we all share bring us closer together. Hanging out before and after the meetings is the social side when we develop the bonds that make us feel comfortable sharing those struggles and going to the functions is where we celebrate those bonds. That is the way it worked for me, getting off my ass and getting to make that new set of friends.

Love you all,
RTT
Phil

January 11, 2012

Good Morning,

The friendships that have developed since I started this journey have brought me blessings I never believed possible. The people who call me friend now are the best friends I can ever remember having. They share with me our burdens, our laughter, our blessings and our heartache. They bring me closer to my family and help me to see the true me, good and bad. I love this new life. Last night they shared with me the greatest gift of all. They shared time and family. Thank you all from the bottom of my heart. My family are my heart and all of you help make up the blood that pumps through it. I have so much gratitude.

Love you all,
RTT
Phil

January 12, 2012

Good Morning,

Last night I had a spiritual awakening about faith and how from time to time I lose some faith when I don't get what I want when I want it. That's when old behaviors start kicking in. I start to push instead of letting things be. If I allow life to happen the same ways I allow the program to happen life goes along so smoothly. It is hard when I see something I find so interesting, so attractive to me that I forget my basic rules this program has taught me. That is another blessing brought to me, self-awareness. I can spot this return of old behavior earlier and earlier, allowing me to stop and put the new behaviors back in place. The good things in life will come in their own time, in their own way. When they do, they are always worth the wait.

Love you all,
RTT
Phil

January 13, 2012

Good Morning,

I allow myself to get offended from time to time by gossip that takes place. When I find myself pointing out the gossipers I realize that I am doing the same as them. The pointing fingers game only feeds upon itself. The only way to stop it is to take a good look at myself and stop my own behavior. If I don't participate that is one less person in the game. Today I will turn my eyes inward and look at the behavior that I need to stop.

Love you all,
RTT
Phil

January 14, 2012

Good Morning,

I read this quote this morning, " I make mistakes; I'll be the second to admit it," and thought it was funny. Thinking about it made me realize, that it was the way I lived my life in my addiction. The idea was to get away with all I could get away with until I got caught. The new idea is to recognize when I make mistakes and be the first to admit to them so that I learn to not make them again. Self-awareness is something I struggle with. Justification before I act was the norm. Now the idea is to realize my thinking is wrong first and then to sort out a healthy and productive means of dealing with my problems. The more aware I am, the more effective I can be. That is taking some time to do. Progress is not perfection.

Love you all,
RTT
Phil

A Glimpse of the Journey

January 15, 2012

Good Morning,

How fortunate are we? For me looking back just a few short months ago I was lost inside my addiction or more appropriately, my head. I thought there was no way out. My world was insane and so were my behaviors. I reacted instead of acted. I blamed instead of accepted. I feared instead of hoped. I still have fears. But, now I face them instead of running from them. I have true friendships and people who I care about on levels I did not know was possible. I care about others' futures and how I affect them. I ask myself strange questions like, "Is what I do going to positively or negatively affect others:" Yes, I am a lucky man. My soul calms more and more everyday and I am able to help myself by helping others instead of only thinking of me. Thank you all for sharing.

Love you all,
RTT
Phil

January 16, 2012

Good Morning,

One of the things that is becoming easier for me is stepping into the unknown. As my faith grows, my fear subsides. The quote today is from Martin Luther King Jr. and it is "Take the first step into faith. You don't have to see the whole staircase, just take the first step." I took my first step when I walked into the rooms the third time. I came once out of desperation, once from coercion and the third time from faith. The first two times I had left feeling better than when I came in and I had faith that at least that much would work again. Anything was better than continuing to feel like that. Little did I know the full benefits. I see people struggling and it hurts. I know their pain. So simple, yet so hard. I have much love for them as they struggle.

Love you all,
RTT
Phil

A Glimpse of the Journey

January 18, 2012

Good Morning,

I had a discussion yesterday with a friend about past lifestyles and behaviors. The way I used to act. The way I used to react. I like the idea of creating each anew. The behaviors I had yesterday can be the same or different. I can choose how I react now. I guess I always had the choice. I just didn't always have the ability. Today I can be as good a person as I choose to be or as bad. When I choose the good, my days are filled with happiness and freedom. When I choose the bad, my nights are long and restless. I prefer to sleep well and wake refreshed than to toss and turn all night. But either way it is my decisions throughout the day that cause those results. I used to sleep pretty good either way till this program and you people helped me to develop a respect for myself and others.

Love you all,
RTT
Phil

January 19, 2012

Good Morning,

The meditation today speaks of turning molehills into mountains. Another of the things I struggle with daily. There are days when I fall into the "woe is me" category, some days it's I'm so lonely, some days it's why am I not appreciated, blah, blah, blah. The truth of the matter is that I have a life full of relationships like I have never known. Friends so incredibly loyal I am shocked. There are voids in my life, but they are small and God will fill them in his own time. The vast expanse of smooth flat ground is abundant and life is better than I have ever known. I fell asleep early last night with my kids happy, with bellies full of the most wonderful chicken noodle soup (home made by a wonderful friend) feeling a bit sorry for myself, feeling unappreciated. When I woke this morning to a bunch of texts from friends wishing me a good night, thanking me for being a part of their day and telling me to sleep well, I realized how foolish I can be and how fortunate I truly am.

Love you all,
RTT
Phil

A Glimpse of the Journey

January 20, 2012

Good Morning,

Most days I make a little progress, my thinking changes a little bit, my behaviors follow suit. My attitude improves and my problem solving skills get a little better. Many times I don't see these little improvements and I get a little frustrated, but they are there. I find out they are there in a rush usually, a situation arises and after it's over I realize that I handled it much differently than I would have in the past. It seems to me that I am not changing, but I am. I am learning relationship skills that affect all areas of m life. I am learning how to be a better friend than I ever was before and I see that because I have friendships than I ever had before. People are more reliable to me because I am more dependable to them. They answer my calls because I answer theirs. I once told a friend of mine, "It's not the size of the step that matters, it's the direction." Learning patience has been the hardest, but the rewards the greatest.

Love you all,
RTT
Phil

January 21 2012

Good Morning,

Quote of the day, "Some cause happiness wherever they go; others whenever they go." Keeping a good positive attitude can be hard for me to do all the time. The support group I looked for and continue to build is full of people who bring happiness wherever they go. Hanging around with these people helps me a lot in improving my attitude. If one of us is down the others all surround them with laugher and many times silliness. A few moments in this type of company spins my mood. They spread positive energy with their clown like behavior or just by the way they care for others. I like to spend time with the people who make my insides smile. When I am around people who are happy, joyous and free, those qualities manifest themselves in my heart and soul. When I first started coming that was a huge factor in bringing me back. Thank god the people in the rooms didn't reject me when they were all happy to see me go. They loved me till I loved myself.

Love you all,
RTT
Phil

January 25, 2012

Good Morning,

I was told so many things when I walked in the rooms: just hang in there, it will get better, in time it will become more and more of a non issue; keep coming back. There were a lot more but most importantly, I love ya. I found that, one of the most difficult to believe. They told me they would love me till I loved myself. I didn't much believe that I could ever love myself again. I thought I might be able to like myself, but love myself? I had forgotten what that felt like. All the things they told me have come true and then some, the rewards of doing the next right thing for the next right reason are immeasurable. The return of self esteem by doing esteemable acts, the return of self confidence by having faith, the return of love by loving others. The rewards amazed me early on and continue to do so.

I love you all,
RTT
Phil

February 2012

February 1, 2012

Good Morning,

The blessings keep pouring in. Isn't fear a strange beast? Blessed with a job and I am excited but also a bit nervous. My support group will be much more difficult to see. I am a little frightened because for 5 years I was unemployable. I chose drugs over everything else. I had many years of employability before that. With HP's help and this new ability to focus I know things will work out just fine. But that crazy fear does its best to sneak and grow inside. I pray for His will to be done.

A Glimpse of the Journey

February 3, 2012

Good Morning,

When I came in the rooms I was told it would get better. I hoped it would get better. I prayed it would get better. Relief, I had to have relief. I was depressed, constantly reminded of the horrible person I was in addiction. I would go to meetings and feel better when I walked out then in. That would last a little while, sometimes only till I got back to the house. But I felt better. The first six months were a grind for me. Little by little I began to feel better. I still carried hatred in my heart, hatred for myself and for my past. But I could see a little daylight. About nine months in, I started to let go of some of that hatred and felt like I could get past the feeling of impending doom. About a year in, I felt as if there might be a future. I have a little over 15 months now and have far surpassed what I thought was possible and it just keeps getting better. The point is it took time. But the rewards far exceeded my wildest dreams.

Love you all,
RTT
Phil

Phil Krause

February 7, 2012

This was sent to me by my daughter this morning. This is one of the benefits of the program. Some of it will make no sense to you. But you get the idea.

"I know there isn't. I can pass spelling dad ☺ ha ha. I love you too and I know you are doing this for us and you also! And you have no idea how proud I am to hear you speak at meetings and help others. That's the reason I love going to them with you because I know they are what is keeping you clean most of all and you clean is a happy family even if mom isn't here with us. I think it is pretty awesome having you as a dad and her as a mom and I'm glad I have a family even if it isn't all together ☺. I love you and I'm proud of you too! ☺ and I'm glad you got a job that is good paying and will help us with money. Haha there is no u in family though! But there is an ily ! ☺. You know I love you dad and will miss you a ton. But I know it's for the best! ☺. And then we can go see COLDPLAY in August ☺ Ehh Ehh? ☺ hahe. ☺ Woohoo! ☺

Love you all,
Phil

A Glimpse of the Journey

February 10, 2012

Good Morning,

I start work today. I have to admit I am a little nervous. It has been a long time. So say a quick prayer for me this morning. With the tools you all have taught me and with a clear head, I know all will be well. I am a lot excited. Ready to turn the page on this new chapter of life and see where it leads. My life has changed so much over the last 16 months. Every change has brought improvement. Every improvement has been a happy one in the end. So, onward to the next change.

I love you all,
RTT
Phil

Phil Krause

February 11, 2012

Good Morning,

This morning I have been thinking about the blessings this new life has bestowed upon me. The relationships I have now with family and friends, the new job, the coping skills I have now, the inner peace and serenity and the open mindedness. AS I thanked my HP for all these gifts I realized that those blessings are just the beginning. I thought about all the changes I get to see in the people I see practicing these principles: People getting their families back, people staying free when they could easily have been incarcerated; the second chances we all have received on life; the ability to face some of life's most difficult challenges with a happy heart. I, for years would dodge responsibility for my actions and now accept them and see my friends doing the same thing. All from doing just a few simple things suggested to me by you people. Thank you for your guidance. Thank you for your patience.

I love you all,
RTT
Phil

February 17, 2012

Good Morning,

I still struggle a bit with resentments and anger. I pray every morning for God to guide my thoughts and actions. I know that anger is not God's will for me. To be of the greatest service to my fellow man and to God, I have to let those go. Sometimes it's easy, other times it can be difficult. These feelings usually occur when I am lonely. So, they have been more frequent since I have been out of town. Meetings help, prayer helps and introspection helps. So I guess what I saying is that I miss you all a lot and look forward to getting home where I can see your faces and give you all hugs.

I love you all,
RTT
Phil

Phil Krause

February 19, 2012

Good Morning,

I woke up this morning to the sound of birds singing outside my window, the feeling that a new dawn is breaking. A new beginning is upon me. I look around and see all my friends starting new lives or enjoying the new lives that have been given. I see opportunity around every corner. The new life I have been given is all thanks to changing the way I think, to opening up, being willing and honest, to believing in something greater than myself and letting that something take the wheel and steer. There came a lot of freedom in understanding I am not in control. There came a lot of relief in letting go. Surrender, I always thought that was a weak word, a weak act, a vision of warriors heads hung low, arms raised beaten and defeated. With that defeat comes a freedom and a strength that I never would have understood with being beaten. Thank you God for the good sound ass kicking. I needed it.

Love you all,
RTT
Phil

February 27, 2012

Good Morning,

The last two weeks have been difficult because I have been away from my family. The one thing I didn't expect was that returning home would also hurt. Being away from the kids I rarely thought about their mother and the heartache that still lies there. Seeing them again brought back the pain of the broken family and the anger and heartache. I understand why she doesn't spend much time with the kids it must hurt her as much as it hurts me. This morning text is not going out to the kids as it usually does. I refuse to hurt them anymore than they have been hurt. I share this with all of you so I can get a grasp on these feelings. So I can share where I am and how I feel. The past is something I can't change. I am working on healing that pain. I thought it would be better than it is by now.

The things I have done make it difficult to deal with this pain, but it is my pain. Not theirs. No matter how hard it is I will get through it.

Love you all,
RTT
Phil

February 27, 2012

Good Morning, today the program has given me the ability to recognize when I am lying to myself, the chance to correct that, and the opportunity to change it.

Love you all,
RTT
Phil

A Glimpse of the Journey

February 28, 2012

Good Morning,

In my past everything I did was in a hurry. I hauled ass to the dopeman. I jumped into everything with both feet. I was in a hurry to get everything. Shit I ran to meetings as fast as I could. My one foot in front of the other was always in rapid procession. I have learned that one foot in front of the other does not mean hurry, it only means forward. Not rushing things gets me where I need to go. Not balls to the wall, gives me the chance to see where I am and gives god the chance to guide me. I always thought if I wasn't running I was plodding. That is also not the case. It can feel that way, but I have learned and been told that I am grounded when I walk. Walking takes me out of the rat race and into life. Smelling the flowers, so to speak has given me the gifts and lets me find the rewards. Simple is good.

Love you all,
RTT
Phil

February 29, 2012

Good Morning,

I like the reading today." Anything is possible." As a friend of mine says, "that's a bold statement." I was told as a child that I could do anything I put my mind to. My ideas of anything have changed. The anythings I would have chased are nothing like the anythings I want now. They are more simple. A happy family and a way to support that family. God keeps providing me with those things. There are things I still desire. Most of all I desire for my kids to believe where I did not. To have faith and desire to pursue their dreams, joy in their hearts to be happy in their work and in their lives knowing that if they just do the task at hand all will be well. That is the most important thing I have learned here. If I just do the next thing put in front of me that everything will be ok. Anything is possible, ANYTHING. That is a bold but so true statement. Hmmm, *anything*.

Love you all,
RTT
Phil

March 2011

March 1, 2011

Good Morning,

I have found it to be of the utmost importance to make sure I am on the inside reaching out, not on the outside looking in. Being a part of, a part of the family, a part of the program, a part of the team. When I participate and reach out to help others I am at peace. When I feel outcast and do nothing about it I am isolating and heading down a dangerous path.

Phil Krause

March 2, 2011

It can be difficult for me to not manipulate things. I have to remind myself of the goal. I have to keep in mind that the idea is to earn all I want, not to manipulate into my hands those things. To let things be as they are supposed to be. I have to give those desires over to god. I am learning, slowly but surely I am keeping my dirty little hand out of it and letting it be what it will be. Praying every morning for god to guide my thoughts and my actions. It works so well and then I see something I want, and I see how I could probably get that if I do this or I do that. I have begun to recognize those moments and stop myself before the act. That's the hard part for me. So it's progress not perfection. I am getting much better than I was. Keeping my todays as clean of clutter as possible so that my yesterdays don't cause guilt and shame that could ruin my tomorrows.

Love you all,
RTT
Phil

A Glimpse of the Journey

March 3, 2011

Good Morning,

Words without actions are just words. Recovery is an action. Friendship is an action. Love is an action. To tell someone you are in recovery is easy. To tell someone you are their friend is easy. To tell someone you want them in your life is easy. When I work a program, when I work on a friendship, when I show I care, words are not nearly as important. Today I will DO the things I talk about. Today I will walk as much or more than I talk.

Love you all,
RTT
Phil

Phil Krause

March 4, 2011

Good Morning,

Seems I just got home and it's time to leave again. I wish I cold stay. I miss my family and friends when gone. My heart aches for home, but my new life awaits in the going. These times are the hardest, spending time with family and friends knowing I have to leave. I know the time will go by quickly once I get started. I get to go, I get to learn, I get to support my family. So I will miss you all while I am gone and look forward to the time I get to see you all again. See you in a couple of weeks.

Love you all,
RTT
Phil

A Glimpse of the Journey

March 5, 2011

Good Evening,

Day one is in the books, just returned from a meeting and the topic was who is an addict. I heard a lot of good things one of which was how that applies to me. I first thought that the first chapter applied to the newcomer, fresh in from the streets. But that chapter talks about me, and a lot of the behaviors I still practice. My mind is clearing but I still have a lot of the old behaviors, isolating when I am lonely …. how stupid is that? Getting angry at things out of my control, yet still me. Progress not perfection. So in the morning I will pray for god's will in my life. In the morning I will practice the things that have been taught to me. Thy will be done. God's not mine. Let him take the lead. I fuck things up when I do it. I ended the day with some excitement. On the way back to the room, the fella that was taking me had a fire in the bed of his truck. Made for an interesting trip. Maybe that was god's way of telling me to keep my fire alive or I may well self destruct.

Love you all,
RTT
Phil

March 6, 2011

Good Morning,

Time to welcome another day. Doing the next task set in front of me and not worrying about what is coming next can be a challenge. My head keeps trying to worry and manipulate how can I be the best, how can I make this the way I want it. When the truth is, if I just do the next task set ahead of me to the best of my ability I will be the best I can be and if that is enough for God who am I to question that. As long as I do my best, no excuses, no BS, just do the best I can, everything seems to work out fine. Better than fine. But the mental battle is greater than half of it. Out performing the old mindset, breaking the old habits that have been ingrained for all those years is the challenge Saying "I can" as opposed to "how can I" is my battle today. So I take my shower, get dressed and head out the door knowing in my heart that if I do the next task set ahead of me, I can. Hope you all have a wonderful day. I can.

Love you all,
RTT
Phil

A Glimpse of the Journey

March 7, 2012

Good Moring,

The silliness of my disease shows itself at the strangest times. When Life is going well it pokes its head out of its hidey-hole just to see if I am not paying attention. Doubts and fears creep into my life, can I perform up to par, will I fall short and feel a fool, what's the point of even trying, etc. Then I go and perform above expectation and receive praise and my head thinks it is unwarranted. My doubts and fears ruled my life for so long. Those surely I can't, no way could I do that, they are going to find out I don't know what I am talking about.

I used to run and hide from those thoughts believing they were true. When I put one foot ahead of the other. When I do whatever comes next, as long as I do my best everything works out just as it is supposed to. I see this happen time and time again. Slowly I am beginning to believe in the process and myself again. The program just keeps working for me.

Love you all,
RTT
Phil

March 8, 2012

Good Morning,

This morning's meditation hit home with me and reminded me of what a friend of mine in the program always says, "self esteem is built through performing esteem-able acts". Self-esteem cannot be found in someone else's actions. It is found in my own actions. Love for my self cannot be found in loving someone else. The love of another has made me feel good in the past, but that feeling was fleeting. There have been times in my past when I confused cockiness for confidence. I am just now starting to find my confidence and to have esteem for myself again. I know I say this a lot. However, it amazes me that as long as I keep doing the next right thing for the next right reason, my life goes along very smoothly. When I start to look for outside influences to change the way I feel about myself I am always let down. No one by myself will improve the way I feel about myself.

Love you all,
RTT
Phil

A Glimpse of the Journey

March 9, 2012

Good Morning,

Last night I went to a really good speaker meeting. The speaker said several things that made a lot of sense to me. Doing the next right thing has been something I work hard on. But I am still lacking faith in the -what comes next department. I am going to paraphrase what she said. This isn't an exact quote but something along the lines of… There are two job openings for my life, there is my job, which is to do the next right thing for the next right reason and there is God's job, which is the outcome of the things I do. The outcome is neither, my job, or any of my business. My job is simply doing the next right thing for the next right reason. Seems there is a lot of freedom in that. I don't have to spend any of my energy, any of my time or any of my money trying to influence the outcome. It will be what it will be. I like that concept, a lot.

Love you all,
RTT
Phil

March 11, 2012

Good Morning,

They say an addict alone is in bad company and that is the hardest thing about being down here. This weekend it has rained all weekend and with no transportation I have been stuck here. It has given me the chance for some introspection and I have learned a few things about myself. Some good, some are things I need to change. One of the things I need to change about myself is confidence. I realized in talking with someone that I knew long ago that I lack self-confidence in some areas. I sometimes feel that I as a person am not worthy of friendship and try to entice people with material things, thinking that surely someone wouldn't like me just for me. That was a difficult thing to realize and also that if someone is spending time with me for the things I can do for them or the things I can give them, do I really want that person as a friend anyway. This trip has been good, learning about myself, and things I need to change about me.

Love you all,
RTT
Phil

A Glimpse of the Journey

March 13, 2012

Good Morning,

Last night I woke up in the middle of the night feeling very left out. Being down here is a challenge. A challenge I will contend with but still a challenge. Everything in work life is going well. I just feel a bit isolated. I have been going to meetings but don't have the connections here that I have at home. I miss my kids and my friends and can't wait to be at a home group meeting. So it's off to tackle another day knowing I have your support but wishing I were closer to it. However 1 week down and 4 to go. Everyday is one step closer. I have been going to meetings almost every day. The group of guys I am here with, are understanding and do their best to get me to meetings. Funny in the short time I have been here even they can spot the days I need one the most.

Love you all,
RTT
Phil

March 14, 2012

Good Morning,

The reading this morning has me thinking about relationships. I have, of course been thinking about the bad ones. I was getting angry and frustrated. My thoughts were on violence and revenge. Then the thought occurred to me that those relationships would never be given the chance to heal if that is where my focus was. Maybe just maybe if I focus on improving the good relationships that I have, give the bad relationships some time and some distance that my God will work on me, and those relationships. If I focus on making the good better, the bad will follow. Raising the bar, if I raise the good to better the average will improve. It seems that way with all things. If I live in the bad, I stay in the bad. If I continued to use, my life got worse. When I quit, my life got better. Will it work the same with relationships? If I live in the good, will all relationships improve? There is still a lot of healing to do. But if I focus on the bad, they will never have a chance.

Love you all

A Glimpse of the Journey

March 15, 2012

Good Morning,

The separation from family and friends being down here is wearing on me. I have always disliked being away from those things I am familiar with. Being outside my comfort zone has given me the opportunity to work on those feelings, to learn to cope through other avenues. I used to cover these feelings with substances. Now I have to find new ways to cope. I go to meetings regularly and have made a few friends. Last night was a little tougher than others. There was a party going on at the pool right in front of my room. The laughter and seemingly good times were messing with me head a bit. I called the kids and friends and connected myself to the ties that bind and took comfort in the fact that I would feel good today. Unlike the partying crowd, that today I'm sure wishes they hadn't partied last night. So I get ready for another day of learning and growth.

Love you all,
RTT
Phil

March 19, 2012

Good morning,

Being down here can be challenging for me. I from time to time feel disconnected. Being away from my kids, I sometimes feel like I am not being the father I should and feel I am not doing all I can do. Last night Curtiss sent me a text and asked what I was doing. When I replied he told me about Roxie being missing all day. Both the kids were very upset and I was as well. My first reaction was to be angry with their Mom for not keeping a better eye on Roxie. But as I thought about it I realized that kind of thinking wasn't going to get me or them anywhere. I sent them a text and suggested we do what we could and not think about what we couldn't do. So I sent out the text and called the people I turn to for help. With great ideas flying and people volunteering right and left my hopes raised. Prayers went out and within a few hours Roxie was found. You people are my lifeline and I love you all.

A Glimpse of the Journey

March 23, 2012

Good Morning

Being grateful for the gifts that God has given me. I like to think I do that. However, I realized while thinking about it I spend too much of my time thinking about the things I have lost and not about the things I have. It is difficult for me. There is something inside me that tells me this is not how it is supposed to be. But it is the way it is. Refocusing is where I struggle. Loneliness is my greatest enemy. There was a time I was very comfortable being alone. That was a long time ago. But if I have done it before, I know I can do it again. Learning how to be comfortable alone without drugs is what I am learning. I always had the high to hide behind, cover up those feelings that used to be the answer. The new answer eludes me. As long as I keep looking inward instead of outward, I will find that spot again. The answer lies in the steps and the steps are in me.

I Love you all,
RTT
Phil

Phil Krause

March 24, 2012

Good Morning,

The past that matters most for me started just over 17 months ago. The rest of it is all stuff I did to get myself ready for the personal history I am makng today. I am grateful for the program, the life it has given me and the ability to see the truth now.

Love you all,
Getting ready to go to the 8 at JFT
RTT
Phil

A Glimpse of the Journey

March 26, 2012

Good Morning,

I had a wonderful trip home. The time spent with my kids was fantastic. Seeing and spending time with them renewed my drive to press o. Knowing that what I going through now will provide for us later. The time I spent with my NA family rejuvenated my enthusiasm for recovery and the blessing it brings into my life. The rewards I reap through the program and the people in it amaze me. The ability to most times stay calm through stressful situations, to understand other people's frustrations, but also to stand up for myself and then stick by my decisions. Many of these attributes are new to me. Having empathy for those who are struggling in their lives. To have compassion for those I would have turned my back on in the past. To laugh at myself when I find I have been wrong or when I have been wronged. Wow what a wonderful life. It's a beautiful day and wonderful things are in store for us.

Love you all,
RTT
Phil

Phil Krause

March 27, 2012

Good Morning

Today I have been thinking that another wonderful benefit of this program is the gift of patience. Having the ability to make decisions after thinking about them. The gift of not having to act before I think. Not being stuck with a decision I wish I hadn't made. What a blessing.

Love you all,
RTT
Phil

A Glimpse of the Journey

March 28, 2012

Good Morning,

The unseen benefit of facing my feelings, for me, was once I started facing them I came to realize that they are not as bad as I made them out to be. Pain still hurts but not as much as I made it hurt before. Fear is still scary, but it no longer causes me to freeze. Sadness is still depressing, but it no longer consumes me. All of this raises the bar on my emotional level. The average of my feelings is much higher or more toward the positive allowing me to be more positive and happier in general. Keeping a positive outlook and being around more generally happy people also helps. I am able to give more of myself to my family and friends when I am happier and more fulfilled. Which in turn brings around a more happy Phil. Just as the things we once did spiraled us out of control. The things we are doing now can lift us up, ever increasing our happiness. Today my life is great and only getting better.

Love you all,
RTT
Phil

Phil Krause

March 30, 2012

Good Morning,

For the last few weeks I have had song lyrics running through my head. Over and over again I find myself singing, "I'm doin' all right getting good grades, the futures so bright I gotta wear shades, I gotta wear shades" thank you God for providing me with this new life and all it's fantastic trimmings.

Love you all,
RTT
Phil

A Glimpse of the Journey

March 31, 2012

Good Morning,

Less than a week and my happy turtle-riding butt will be home. Today I am helping a fellow addict move from Dallas to Houston. I have a high school friend who lives in Houston that I may try to see while I am there. It is a beautiful day today and I am fortunate enough to be clean and living a life in recovery. What a great day to be alive. Life is going great and it's only getting better

Love and miss you all,
RTT
Phil

April 2012

April 2, 2012

Good Morning,

Last night I woke up in the middle of the night by a very vivid nightmare that was full of violence. It was very real and very scary for me. I have had nightmares in the past that were scary but this one scared me in a different kind of way. I was the person committing the violence. It really disturbed me. I don't like scary movies and when they are playing in my head they are even worse. I woke up panicked and wondering where I was going to hide a body. It took a couple of hours for me to calm down and realize it was only a dream and that all was well. I decided to look at it like I would any other dream and understand they are only thoughts and as long as I don't act on them all will remain fine. I have moments now when Peace eludes me. But they are just moments. It used to be that peace was the rarity. Now my life is great and just keeps getting better.

Love you all
RTT

A Glimpse of the Journey

April 4, 2012

Good Morning,

Last night I went to a meeting, great meeting. I found myself sharing with others the things I needed to hear. Funny how that works. I have two nights left ….. TWO. I am very excited to get home and see everyone, mostly my kids. I miss them so much. They are my life. See you all soon.

Love to you all
Phil

April 17 2012

Good Morning,

I woke up this morning feeling a little down. I prayed for God's guidance in my life. I prayed for him to guide my thoughts and my actions. Sometimes I forget just how lucky I am. I have my kids in my life. I am alive. I am not wasting my money on drugs. I have money. I have a job. I have all the things I need and most of what I want. My life is great and only getting better. I have to remember that.

Love you all
RTT
PHIL

A Glimpse of the Journey

April 18, 2012

Good Morning,

Keeping my side of the street clean….just MY side of the street clean is of the utmost importance. I don't have to worry about anyone else's side of the street, just mine. That frees a lot of my time up to do the right things for the right reasons. Finding out the world doesn't revolve around my ass is quite a relief. No longer is it my job to see to it that people are doing things the way I think they should.

Love you all
RTT
Phil

April 20, 2012

Good Morning,

My side of the street, leave everyone else's street alone. Pushing on someone else to do what I think is the right thing to do creates resentment, anger and hostility. Doing right things and living as right as I can shows others there is another way. It is their decision to do what they want with that information.

Love you all,
RTT
Phil

April 21, 2012

Good Morning,

Today I will be missing the morning meeting I enjoy so much and heading into work. The program has helped me become employable again. Now it's my job to show others this program works by being a responsible acceptable and productive member of society. Soooooooooo. Hi Ho Hi Ho it's off to work I go.

Love ya all
RTT
Phil

April 24, 2012

Good Morning,

I worked hard yesterday, went to bed early and woke with a soreness in my muscles, laid in bed longer than usual thinking I hope I get an easy day today. I thought to myself then, what was easy about my addiction? I ran and chased, hustled and lied, lost time with my family and lost some of my family. Nothing about those days was easy. Today it is my responsibility to keep my perspective right. It is my job to keep a positive frame of mind. It is my job to go and do my job.

Love you all,
RTT
Phil

A Glimpse of the Journey

April 25, 2012

Good Morning,

I have good problems today. I have responsible acceptable productive problems today. The problems I face are those of a normal nature. Waking up sore from a hard day's work. Dealing with kids with poor performance at school. Kids being bored at home or wanting to go and do something else when I am tired. Teenage daughter with a boyfriend problems. They have nothing to do with law enforcement problems, or house raiding problems, or I am out of dope problems, not even a where am I going to get enough money to get enough dope to get out of bed problems. I gladly face the problems I have today because they are good problems.

Love you all
RTT
Phil

April 27, 2012

Good Morning,

I spent some time with a friend last night and we talked about the desire to get clean and stay clean. What causes that spark in someone? What brought about that desire? The desire in someone else is something I have no control over. I can't light the fire. I can however kindle that flame. I can offer my emotional support. I can give someone a ride to a meeting. I can offer my ear and I can pray for that person. I wish there were magic words to say that would turn on the light and let others see through the darkness. If this shit were easy everyone would be doing it. Not everyone does. Not everyone wants to. This is not a program for pussies. It is a program of progress, sometimes painfully slow progress. But that's ok. It matters not the size of the step, just the direction. Today I will pray for those that are lost in the dark. It may well be the best and only thing I can do for them.

I Love you all,
RTT
Phil

A Glimpse of the Journey

April 30, 2012

Good Morning,

Today I am grateful for my job and the feeling of fulfillment it brings. I am grateful for my family. I am grateful that the kids' Mom is taking a more active role in their lives. I am grateful that this town has the great recovery it has and I am grateful for all of you.

Love you all,
RTT
Phil

May 2012

May 2, 2012

Good Morning,

Today I have the day off work. I get to go to my 8 am meeting and see people I don't get to see very often anymore. Yeaaaaa. I also have a list of things to accomplish today but the most important thing I have to do today is spend time with friends. All the other stuff is mandatory, but staying connected to all of you is what saves my life. So today I tend to the mandatory and get to enjoy the life saving. I am so grateful to have all of you as my support system.

I Love you all,
RTT
Phil

A Glimpse of the Journey

May 3, 2012

Good Morning,

Practicing the principles of this new life can be difficult. Patience has been the most difficult. Building the faith that HP will provide .... I was told as a child that if I wanted something to put my head down and push. But it seems the more I pushed the farther away the things I wanted became. So I practice patience. Sometimes I do well and other times I fall back on the old behavior. So I practice. Slowly the faith builds. I see improvement so I practice more. I hope each and everyone of you has the most wondrous day, filled with joy and happiness.

Love you all,
RTT
Phil

May 4, 2012

I have to get emotion under control. Think it's about time to work some steps on that.

Love you all,
RTT
Phil

A Glimpse of the Journey

May 10, 2012

Good Morning,

I see changes in my life. I am becoming a better father than I have ever been. That part is hard for me. I want to be my kids' friend all the time and there are times when that is not the best thing to do. I talked to my kids last night and sounded so much like my Dad that it scared me. I didn't like the feeling. But I also know that without guidance and consequences I would be doing them a dis-service. Their lives are more important than my feeling like their friend for a few days. So many changes: work is going well and I feel good about the way I now handle my business, plenty of room for improvement but I feel better about it than I ever have in the past. Accepting my place in this world is bringing me peace. Being who I am supposed to be instead of being something I'm not is bringing serenity.

I Love you all,
RTT
Phil

May 11, 2012

Good Morning,

The challenges of raising a teenage girl can be overwhelming sometimes. Not understanding women and trying to understand a teenage woman, wanting to be fair, wanting to be open minded ….. arrrrhg. I do the best I can, leading by example can be difficult. Old behaviors want to rear their ugly heads. Sometimes I feel like I am playing whack a mole with my defects. Practice, practice, practice. That's all I can do. So I ask God to guide my thoughts and actions today. Lord knows I need it.

Love you all,
RTT
Phil

A Glimpse of the Journey

May 14, 2012

Good Morning,

I heard a saying yesterday that made some sense. It goes something along the lines of …. there are two dogs inside of me, a good dog and a bad dog … which one is bigger? The one I feed the most.

Today I choose to feed the good dog.

Have a great day
I Love you all,
RTT
Phil

Phil Krause

May 15, 2012

Good Morning,

Watching my kids grow up is an amazing adventure. Bailey turns 16 today and it seems just yesterday I was watching her run around pigtails bouncing around, singing Bobby McGee. Where has the time gone? The good thing is from now forward I have the choice to remember. I have the choice to be in their lives. Through this program I have the chance to be the father these kids deserve.

I Love you all,
RTT
Phil

May 16, 2012

Good Morning,

From time to time the serenity eludes me. Usually when I seek it the hardest is when it plays hide and seek. Just letting life happen is the easiest way for me to find it. Getting mad fucks with my Chi. I would rather not have that fucked with. The things I have to remember is I am the only one who can influence that. Others may create obstacles. I must find a gentle path around them and move on.

Love you all,
RTT
Phil

May 17, 2012

Good Morning,

I woke up this morning and immediately had negative thoughts. Then I received a text from a friend in the program that made me realize just how fortunate I am. How lucky I am to have my kids in my life, a good job that I enjoy doing, fantastic friends who love and support me, a father who is forgiving and kind and a program that guides me to this gratitude. Focus on the good. Feed the good dog.

I Love you all,
RTT
Phil

A Glimpse of the Journey

May 17, 2012

Good Evening,

Sorry this one couldn't wait till the morning. So I go downtown to pick up my daughter and I park in front of the outland ballroom to wait for her. I am there just a few minutes listening to music and waiting, a cop pulls up next to me and rolls down his window looking at me. I am not worried but think to myself ... now what. So I roll down the window and he says, "LOVE THE BRONCO, what is that a '91?" Gotta love this new life and the simple joys it brings.

Good night everyone,
Sweet dreams to you all
Love each and every one of you.
RTT

May 19, 2012

Good Morning,

This work thing is improving so many areas of my life. Seeking the balance can be challenging but the self esteem, the feeling of satisfaction of doing a good job and the relief of having money again, blessed in many ways with the whole job thing. My life is slowly balancing out and I like it.

Once again hope to see you all at coffee tomorrow morning at Classic Rock at 8, then it's off to Ron's for the men's breakfast.

Love you all,
RTT
Phil

A Glimpse of the Journey

May 21, 2012

Good Morning,

Today I am grateful that I have a choice how I live my life. I didn't used to. I used to react to others' actions. I still fight the old behaviors. I still want to react. But today I don't have to. So I practice living the way I want to live. I do my best to live by those spiritual principles that I was once so unfamiliar with. I think about how I want to live, and how my actions will be perceived by others. Are they acceptable actions? If not I need to change the way I feel about things to be an acceptable, responsible and productive member of this society. I like peace and tranquility in my life now. I dislike confrontation but I will not be someone's doormat. I get to vote with my feet, leave them to their own devices and ways.

I Love you all,
RTT
Phil

Phil Krause

May 22, 2012

Good Morning,

I love the spiritual awakenings I have had. I am not fond of the pain that usually precedes them. But that is a necessary part of the learning process for me. It seems that I refuse to change unless I suffer some kind of painful consequence. It would be very nice to be able to say to myself, "I really should stop messing around with these crazy bitches first, and then I will let them go. That is the way it is for me with most things: drugs, sloth, etc. etc. I have to learn through pain or frustration. Maybe someday with practice I will learn to spot my downfalls before I have to suffer. Until then ….. bring on the crazy bitches? I guess. No I am swearing off of them ….. RIGHT!

Love you all,
RTT
Phil

A Glimpse of the Journey

May 24, 2012

Good Morning,

Learning I am vulnerable ... not letting others see I am vulnerable has been humbling. I have always known I am vulnerable. I tried to hide it or ran from the feelings because I thought it was a sign of weakness. It can be difficult to not resort to my old survival habits, especially in times of stress. When my feelings are hurt, I don't want to appear weak for fear of being attacked. I always lived by the rule, "a good defense is have a good offense". So I practice allowing others to know how I feel. I allow my friends and family to see my weaknesses now. Finding out that I am human allows them to be human as well. I always hated crying in times of stress, never realized it was not out of fear, but out of being the person I didn't want to be, of containing emotions that should have been talked out or worked through. I was criticized for crying by my peers and told it was weakness. I now know differently. I was a being human and that is a good thing.

Love you all,
RTT
Phil

May 26, 2012

Good Morning,

I get to work this morning (not feeling it right now, but that will change when I get there and get moving). I pray this morning for guidance in my thoughts and actions today. So that I may be the man God would have me be. I pray that I may look upon others with eyes closer to God's than my own. See people through kind and loving eyes, understanding they have problems just like I do and they are doing their best as well. I will be missing seeing you all at the meetings today, but hope that I get the chance to stop by winner's circle picnic this evening.

A Glimpse of the Journey

May 25, 2012

Good Morning,

Strange to me I used to avoid work as much as possible, would think of reasons and ways to avoid it. Now I wake up feeling a little lazy but tell myself that I know I will feel better when I get moving and find once I am at work, that there is a sense of accomplishment and a feeling of serenity in the labors of the day. I actually enjoy it. When payday comes and I am putting more money in the bank than I am spending, I enjoy that as well. This bring a productive, acceptable, responsible member of society thing is pretty cool. I was at work the other day and another addict happened to drive by, stopped and told me he was proud of me. People proud of me, that's something that is a new and enjoyable feeling. The changes come slowly but are worth the wait. Lots more growing to do, think I will go do some. Off to work.

Love you all,
RTT
Phil

Phil Krause

May 27, 2012

Good Morning,

Yesterday I picked up an install of a type I had not done before. This type of install is known to be difficult and very time consuming. I started to feel intimidated and my mind started down the, I will fail at this path. During the drive to the house I thought to myself, "this is an opportunity to learn how" and prayed for guidance and to look at this as a chance to learn and grow.

Everything started as well as it could and then became problematic. I made a phone call or two and before I knew it, one of the other techs with much more experience showed up on my job, having left his job in the middle to offer some guidance and get me over the hump. The job finished well and I left having learned a lot and having found a new resource for information. This morning the daily meditation was about just that, facing challenges with a new outlook. Made me think, " maybe ... just maybe ... I might be starting to understand how this new life works".... maybe.

Love you all,
RTT
Phil

May 29, 2012

Good Morning,

My faith grows day by day. I practice this new life to the best of my ability and when I do the right things for the right reasons I see positive things happening in my life. I do what is right by my family and friends. I do my best to act appropriately in every situation. I patiently wait when I need to. I do my best to think through my decisions as often as I can. When I have doubts about what is appropriate, I seek counsel from those around me that I trust, make my decision and move on. I was called a bully yesterday because of the way I parent my kids. I thought about that quite a bit yesterday, worried over my actions and then reach out to those in my support network and asked advice. I realized that as much as I don't like imposing consequences on my children for their behavior, I would be doing them a dis-service if I didn't. Made my decision and moved on. This new life is liberating and I like it.

Love you all,
RTT
Phil

June 2012

June 2, 2012

Good Morning,

This work thing sure is getting in the way of my meeting attendance. I miss my meetings but the fulfillment I get from working and being a productive, acceptable, responsible member of society fills most of the void. I feel a bit isolated sometimes but I know you are all still there for me. That feeling is a huge part of my stability and ability to keep on keeping on. The changes that are occurring in me and my life have all been positive. I see the difference in all aspects of my life and I appreciate them and all of you.

Love you all,
RTT
Phil

A Glimpse of the Journey

June 3, 2012

Good Morning,

This morning's reading held special meaning for me. Making indirect amends, changing the way I act. There are people in my life I have made direct amends to who don't want to hear those words from me. So I change the way I act, making living amends. By being honest I make living amends to those I have lied to. By being open minded I make living amends to those I shut out, listening to what they say and giving serious thought to their ideas. By being willing I make living amends to those I have taken advantage of. By doing my best to live a life of service, being a better father to my children, by being a better son to my father, by being a better friend to my friends, living a better life for all those I care about I clean my side of the street. And that brings peace and harmony to my life.

Doing good things brings good karma.

Love you all,
RTT
Phil

June 4, 2012

Good Morning,

Just a little progress every day. It's funny how often the voodoo book (the morning mediation) talks about the things I need to hear. It used to be maybe a day ahead or right on track with the things I need to hear. These days it seems I am a day ahead of it. These small amounts of progress build into the life I strive for. Yesterday I was in the position of choosing to be spiteful and mean, or to let that go and do something that benefits others. I decided to do for others. Today I don't regret the things I did yesterday. I feel good about the way my day went and look forward to today. So it's time to jump in the shower, put more faith in the god of my understanding and face my day with a new hope for better things ahead.

Love you all,
RTT
Phil

A Glimpse of the Journey

June 5 A & B

A.

Good Morning,

I have been fighting this feeling of being disconnected lately. I know it's associated with work and not being able to spend as much time with my kids and not being able to hit meetings like I used to. I also know if I fight for balance, it eludes me. So once again patience, acceptance and faith are key. Staying focused, doing the next right thing for the next right reason will carry me through. So today I hope for god to guide my thoughts and actions, allowing me to see others through his eyes not my own so that I may become the man he would have me be.

Love you all,
RTT
Phil

B.

Good morning again,

This morning as I said before I was and have been feeling disconnected from my kids and meetings. I got up anyway and headed in to work. When I walked in the door they asked if I wanted the day off. (Smile) Yes. Yes, I do. So I am going to take care of a few things, hit a meeting and then go spend some time with my kids. My god knows what I need and supplies it when I do need it.

Love you all,
Love this new life
RTT
Phil

A Glimpse of the Journey

June 6, 2012

Good Morning,

I had a great day yesterday. I was able to spend some quality time with my kids. I am so blessed to have such wonderful kids. Watching Curtiss overcome his fears and enjoy the zipline made my chest fill with pride, riding back seat of the car as Baily drove us down to Branson did too. They are growing so fast. I realized that Bailey drives like I do ... HOLY SHIT HANG ON! It was truly a blessing to get the time with them. I was able to catch a couple of meetings and regain some of the connection I felt I had lost. What a wonderful day. So today it's back in the saddle and off to work I go.

Love you all,
Have a great day.
RTT
Phil

June 7, 2012

Good Morning,

I woke up this morning clean. No matter what else is going on, and the things that are going on today are good. Even if they were bad, I woke up clean this morning. And that is a very good indication of how my life is going. The decisions I make today are small corrections to my course. No more jerking the wheel from side to side seeking the right course. Small corrections mean small deviations from where I want to be. Small corrections insure I am headed in mostly the right direction. I like where I am heading if I stay the course. My life is great and keeps getting better.

Love you all,
RTT
Phil

P.S. take that woody,
you didn't wake me up today. HA. ;-)

A Glimpse of the Journey

June 8, 2012

Good Morning,

Working this weekend and hoping to make it up to the pig roast on Saturday, maybe. Have fun and I will do my best to make it up there. Time to be acceptable, productive and responsible.

Love you all,
Phil

June 9, 2012

Good Morning,

My friends are all up at the pig roast and I would love to be there with them. However a big part of this program also includes being an acceptable, responsible and productive part of society. So today I work. Tonight if I get off early enough, I can visit and play with my kids, my friends, my family.

Love you all,
(OK I'm a bit jealous) but that too shall pass.
RTT
Phil

A Glimpse of the Journey

June 13, 2012

Good Morning,

I look at my life today and realize I have good problems. My days no longer consist of running and chasing dope. They no longer consist of wondering where I will get the money to get more dope. I still run and chase. But now I run and chase after life, run and chase after the good things that I want to fill it. My days are now filled with family and friends, filled with acceptable behaviors that won't kill me. I have my bad days, all up in my head, but these bad days are wonderful compared to the bad days I had before. I may feel sad sometimes or lonely. I may feel happy or excited, but none of these feelings are distorted by drugs. None of these feelings are created by a mind warped by a destructive lifestyle. Now, they are created by my own head, and that part of me is getting better all the time, less of the old me, and more of the new me. Growth and change are filling my life and God is filling the holes I created in my addiction.

Love you all,
RTT
Phil

June 14, 2012

Good Morning,

I enjoy faith I have learned and as long as I nurture that faith and my connection to HP, all will be well. I have been worrying over some small things. Expectations have me on edge. What will be will be. Patience and faith will carry me through.

Love you all,
RTT
Phil

A Glimpse of the Journey

June 16, 2012

Good Morning,

Accepting the things I can't change is a struggle for me now and again. The things I can change is a matter of patience. They change slowly over a period of time. Slowly being the key word in that sentence. Things change sometimes so slowly that they don't' seem to be changing at all. Having faith that things are getting better is hard especially during the rough times. I have always been impatient. I expected my life to be better right from the very beginning of my recovery. It has taken time. It is changing for the better though, all the time. Good days and bad days, they both come and go. The miracle is that I don't have to destroy myself by getting high over the bad days and I don't have to celebrate by getting high over the good days. I don't have to get high ever again.

Phil

June 25, 2012

Good Morning,

Last night was a trying one. My daughter has decided to move in with her mother. She is old enough to decide where she wants to live. This followed my decision to take the car away after she broke the rules about when she could drive the car. I understand why she is moving. Life can be a challenge. Spiritual principles were not plentiful during the incident between her mother and me. I do the best I can when I can. I know it will all work out as it's supposed to. So today I pray for God's will in my life, pray for acceptance and faith. The time with her Mom will be a good thing. She has been missing her.

So it's off to work. Try to focus on the task at hand.

Love you all,
Phil

A Glimpse of the Journey

June 27, 2012

Good Morning again,

I keep hearing about people falling, wanting to do something. The only thing I know to do is to fight my own fight, lead by example, show it can be done. It hurts but I am powerless. Keep up the good fight my friends. The enemy is always at our doorstep, constant vigilance.

I Love you all,
Phil

June 28, 2012

Good Morning,

Changes occur slowly over a period of time. The room for growth in me is huge. I still find myself reverting to old behaviors in times of stress. The shock of an unplanned for event sometimes takes me by surprise, and my reactions are not what they should be. Those are the times I find myself falling back into the old ways of dealing with stress. Those are the times I need to slow down and realize that I don't have to make something happen. If I take the time to breathe and evaluate, I can come up with a resolution without the old me rearing it's ugly head. I know those survival mechanisms are long engrained but if I don't change the way I act I don't change the way I think in those times of stress I will never truly change. Slowly over a period of time. So today I pray for God to guide my thoughts and my actions. Guide me today, lord to be the man you would have me be.
Love you all,
Phil

A Glimpse of the Journey

June 29, 2012

Good Morning family,

Another beautiful day. I used to hide from this kind of weather, now it is what it is. I have a job and it just so happens to be in the heat. It pays my bills, helps me to provide for my family and it helps me to be a productive, responsible and acceptable part of this society. So it's time to cleanup, get dressed and show up. And, I am grateful I get to do so. Life is good and only getting better.

Love you all,
Phil

Phil Krause

June 30, 2012

Good Morning,

I love the mornings when I wake up and feel a closer connection to my friends, my family and my HP. Just a sense of serenity, like all is well in the world. The feeling of being on an even keel. Have a wonderful day everyone.

Love you all,
Phil

A Glimpse of the Journey

July 2012

July 10, 2012

Good Morning,

Today my attitudes are changing. Today I do my best to not act in a selfish manner. Today I look at the opportunity to act positively, to see things in a manner. To focus on what's right not when is right for me. These days change is good. Work is an opportunity not a chore. It can be a challenge, but it is a chance to learn and to grow in how I handle myself. I love my life and the way it is changing.

I love you all and an grateful for you.
Phil

July 13, 2012

Good Morning,

Long hours at work and lord knows I need a meeting. Chin up, read my literature and keep an open contact with HP and I will make it. The morning text helps a lot. I am so glad I built a base of friends that keep my going.

Love you all
Hope to see you tonight.
Phil

A Glimpse of the Journey

July 18, 2012

Good Morning,

The desperation of a life so horribly wrong led me to this path. For that I am grateful. Recovery saved my life and saved me from my life.

Love you all,
Phil

July 19, 2012

Good Morning,

My life is full now and my dreams are coming true. In god's time, with patience good things happen.

Love you all,
Phil

A Glimpse of the Journey

July 21, 2012

Good Morning,

The wealth of experience I have at my fingertips is vast. I have willing mentors to show me how and sometimes how not to do life. All I have to do is be willing to listen and take action towards the life of my dreams. If I want to be successful I can start by listening and acting AS IF I am successful.

Love you all,
Phil

July 22, 2012

Good Afternoon,

On the way to the lake, have a flat on the scoot. Love this new life where I don't have to see the bad, get to sit and talk, spend time, laugh and joke. Sitting in the shade, waiting on Dad and the trailer. Amazing the changes in my thoughts and actions.

A Glimpse of the Journey

July 23, 2012

Good Morning,

I am never sure I am living in god's will. I do know that when I try to live in my will things go terribly wrong. When I relax and let things happen my life goes along smoothly. I believe in a power greater than myself. I believe that power wants good things to happen for me. So if I let things happen and things are going well in my life, whoever's will I am living in, is good. That's when I feel as if I am living in god's will.

Love you all,
Phil

July 27, 2012

Good Morning,

If I had set my expectations of what recovery would give me as my goals, I would have sold myself short. Life just keeps getting better.

A Glimpse of the Journey

July 31, 2012

Good Morning,

If we always do what we always did, we will always get what we always got. Taking my inventory let's me see the patterns in my behavior that lead me down the same old paths again and again.

Time to change has come.

Love you all
Phil

July 31, 2012

God please guide my thoughts and my actions today. Give me the strength to practice your will not my own. Help me to be the man you would have me be. AMEN

All is well just working and praying.

August 2012

August 3, 2012

Good Morning,

It's hard to believe that us, this group of maladjusted, liars, cheats and thieves is our best hope of recovery. But it's true. Without all of you, I would not be where I am today. My support group is made up of the best fuckups I have ever met. We all know how not to act and do our best to not act that way.

Love each and every one of you and there is nothing you can do about it.

Phil

Phil Krause

August 4, 2012

Good Morning,

Been fighting the summer time funk, sinuses, cough, etc. etc. Feeling better than I did yesterday. Before I would have called in sick and done nothing with the time, felt guilty about not going and worried if it would effect my job security. I felt worse yesterday and I survived. So I would imagine today I can do the same. So into the shower I go so I can continue to be a responsible, acceptable and productive member of society. Life on life's terms.

Love ya all.

August 6, 2012

Good Morning,

Inner peace. In all areas of my life but one, I have found inner peace. I no longer struggle with the desire to use. I no longer struggle with work ethic. The hardest battle for me in my life now is in the area of relationships. After being heart hurt, I find myself struggling with trust. I seem to look for the things that are going to destroy what I want the most instead of accepting things as they are. Fear grips me when I feel my heart grow ties. My past has been full of abandonment. To grow, to find love again, I have to let that past go. I begin to hold on too tight. To me, it's odd that the woman I want in my life I want to be loving, kind, independent, strong, self-sufficient. Yet when a woman starts to display those traits, I feel the fear of loss creeping in.

So I turn back to the steps and another hard look at myself and the why's of why I act and feel the way I do.

Love you all,
Phil

August 7, 2012

Good Morning,

Today I am grateful for wonderful kids. Their love and support have been paramount in my recovery. I am grateful for my friends in the program who are always there with an ear and their suggestions. I am grateful for my job and the security and feelings of accomplishment that it provides. I am grateful for my Dad and all his support. He is a cornerstone of my recovery. I am grateful for the daily reminders I get in the literature and on my phone to be grateful for the things I do have.

Love you all,
Phil

A Glimpse of the Journey

August 9, 2012

Good Morning,

I sometimes wonder where the lesson is and then it usually gets answered by the voodoo book and by my support group. Looking for love in all the wrong places. Expect to find love where it has always been…all around me. So today I will look to my higher power for the love to fill the void. I will not expect others to be more than they are. I will accept things the way they are and be happy the lessons are taught, not ask why they are taught. Seeing things in a different light. Change my perspective. Change my life.

Love you all,
Phil

August 10, 2012

Good Morning,

Prayer and Meditation are a morning ritual of mine. I pray for God to guide my will and my life so that I may be of the greatest service to him and to my fellow man. Some days I need guidance towards service, and others I need it away from what I think is service. I find it difficult to find the middle ground. It makes me feel good to be helpful. I have to remember that others need to do things on their own for their growth as well. If I stand in their way, I am a hindrance.

A Glimpse of the Journey

August 14, 2012

Good Morning,

As I continue to focus on relationships, this morning's reading holds special meaning. The idea that I needed someone else to be whole, and searching for that whole person is crazy. Every time I have found a relationship worth having it fell in my lap when I wasn't looking. I seem to forget that, when I get lonely. It seems that cycle is the most difficult for me to break. Time to chill out. Enjoy this time. I went on a date a few days ago with nothing more on my mind than just having a nice time. That is what I got, a nice time, a nice ride and an evening of laughter. Kept my expectations out of it and just enjoyed the evening. I had forgotten how much fun that is. Think I will do that some more.

Love you all,
Phil

August 15, 2012

Good Morning,

As I drove to work I saw a beautiful sunrise and I thought to myself how grateful I am to see those things again, to notice the wonder of life around me. I have a great life now. All the things are falling back in place, not all at once, but slowly over a period of time. Seeing others and myself bathed in the warm soft glow of this new life. My perspective is changing all the time. I get to decide how I feel about my life, my work, my relationships. I can choose to look with old eyes or new ones. I prefer the new ones. Slowly ever a period of time. Progress seems to take forever. But when I take the time to reflect on the who I was and the who I am, it is all well worth the wait. It just keeps getting better if I let it.

Love you all,
Phil

A Glimpse of the Journey

August 16, 2012

Good Morning,

If I am standing still, I am really moving backwards. Growth and change are constant. Do I want to grow spiritually or do I want to lose the progress I have made. I choose growth.

Love you all,
Phil

August 21, 2012

Good Morning,

The friendships I have been blessed with in this new life are amazing. My relationships with these people blossomed because two people decided to care enough about each other to not worry if what we said offended you if you needed to hear it.

Sometimes my problem is I think you need to hear stuff that maybe you don't need to hear, and sometimes I am not ready to hear what others have to say. Thanks to all of those who have over looked that shortcoming of mine and thanks to all of you who said what you thought you needed me to hear no matter what. I have learned to accept other's thoughts and feelings. Slowly over a period of time.

Love you all,
Phil

A Glimpse of the Journey

August 23, 2012

Good Morning,

Making good decisions …. I think that through the program I am making better decisions …. most of the time. The decisions I make are most definitely improved from the ones I used to make. I have better resources and I am willing to seek counsel on difficult decisions I have to make. I have better tools than I had before. I still make choices I wish I hadn't made. But I live with the consequences better than before. I understand that no one is to blame but myself for any circumstance I find myself in…good or bad. I woke up this morning feeling tired and beat down. I know the best decision for me to make is to get up, go to work and it will all be alright. So that's what I am going to do. Have a wonderful day.

Love you all,
Phil

Phil Krause

August 27, 2012

Good Morning,

I enjoy taking care of people and I enjoy being taken care of. I sometimes forget that I can take care of myself just as well as I can take care of others. The superman cape works just as well for myself as it does for others. I have to keep myself saved if I want to be of service.

Love you all
Phil

A Glimpse of the Journey

August 30, 2012

Good Morning,

Today I will remember to treat others as I would like to be treated. Geez, why didn't I listen in kindergarten. Seems this is stuff they covered back then: be kind to your fellow man, do no harm to others. Be compassionate. As we see others not follow those same rules it can be difficult to stay the path. Silly human pride gets in the way. That's why I pray for guidance. I pray for god to make his will apparent to me. I try to consider others feelings. but still be straight forward and frank. I do my best to treat others as I would like to be treated. I also have to remember that others may not want to be treated as I do and when they don't it may be time to create some distance.

Love you all,
Phil

August 31, 2012

Good Morning,

The reading says anything is possible. Anything. I haven't had the feeling that anything is possible in a long time. No restrictions on myself or others. If I stay clean, go to meetings, be of service, work with my sponsor and maintain a personal connections with my HP anything is possible. Seems like a pretty easy recipe to anything. The program has told me that I would lose the compulsion to use, that my life would improve. All those things are happening. So why not "anything is possible"? It's certainly worth a shot.

Love you all,
Phil

September 2012

    September 1, 2012

Good Morning,

My values are constantly changing, the focus becomes less on me and more on others .... That's about it today. I got nothing more. Time for work and a happy day.

Love you all.
Phil

Phil Krause

September 2, 2012

Good Morning,

Last night I went to church. I went to say Hi to a friends and stayed because of what the preacher was saying. Becoming a better person through a connection to God. A connection with higher power brings peace and harmony to my life. The connection I have built has improved me and in turn my life has improved. I ask for guidance every morning and I get it. I fall short of the goal of being as good a person as I would like to be. I make remarks and behave in a way that needs to change. But I do those things a lot less frequently than I ever did before. I am improving. I have tried in the past with little success. But with guidance I am improving. Think I will continue to walk this path and see how much better it can get.

Love you all,
Phil

September 3, 2012

Good Morning,

Humility through anonymity was very difficult for me in the beginning. I was so damaged, my ego was so bruised I used anything to make myself feel better about me. I have noticed that the subject of my recovery doesn't come up as often as it used to. I used to talk about my past with most of my customers at work. I used to bring up the life I used to lead and the things I went through on every job. I still talk about it here and there but not nearly as much as I used to. I have noticed many changes in me. My self-confidence is returning. My ego is healing. I have a sense of self-value that I have not had in a long time. I am once again happy to be me. Looking in the mirror and happy I am looking at that guy. I once again say to my reflection "you good looking SOB, don't you ever die". lol

Love you all,
Phil

September 5, 2012

Good Morning,

I have seen many with some clean time lose their way. It hurts to watch. I know now that I don't have to follow that road. I make a decision to do whatever it takes to not use. Rarely does the thought stay in my head for long. If it lingers I get out of my head, I pray and help others or go to a meeting, anything it takes to not put mind-altering chemicals in my body. With God's help and the help of the people in the program I don't have to ever use again.

Today is a beautiful day, free of the obsession, free to be "not hopelessly bad".

Love you all,
Phil

A Glimpse of the Journey

September 8, 2012

Good Morning,

The voodoo book spoke about being rebellious this morning. I deal with that daily. Last night I showed my ass to my boss. Thank the lord that man and I get along. But just the same I showed my rebel side a bit. So today I think I need to check my attitude, remember to be grateful. I have a job I enjoy doing. The work can be hard and the days can be long. But I really do enjoy what I do. I am blessed daily in that I get to meet some wonderful people. I get to see my friends from time to time, (yeah I am talking about you, ya big sissy). And being a rebel put me right here, staying a rebel will leave me right here. Time to move on from that attitude. I like where I am heading. It keeps getting better. Time to serve instead of being served.

Love you all,
Phil

September 12, 2012

Good Morning,

New horizons abound in my life. The chance for new ways of life, improved and new relationships. It started as soon as I quit using and started living, giving myself to see these new opportunities and new ways of thinking. The promise of a better life was hidden behind old thought and old obsessions. Thank you God for the chance and thank you for opening my eyes.

Love you all,
Ride the turtle
Phil

A Glimpse of the Journey

September 15, 2012

Good Morning,

Today I am driving up to the lake. My sister and her family are going to be there and I haven't seen them in 5 years or so. When my Dad told me they were coming, I was excited to see my nieces and my brother in law. But through a strained relationship, I was neither hot or cold when it came to seeing my sister. Now the day has arrived and through these past few weeks, I have experienced a range of emotion. The history my sister and I have has weighed heavily on my mind. Old emotions, old thought processes have been rushing past. The what if she says this or how will I react to that stuff has been a burden. Then I thought to myself if she brings up the past I am going to tell her, "that man has nothing to do with the man that stands here now" and then I thought the woman who will be standing in front of me may have nothing to do with the person she was either.

Time for an open mind. We may never have the relationship I would like to have with a sibling. But the one we do have can be improved upon. A lot of that improving can be done by continuing to live this new way of life. Much has improved just by living this new way of life. Perhaps this will improve as well. Maybe it won't. But either way it will be all right.

Love you all,
Phil
RTT

Phil Krause

September 17, 2012

Good Morning,

This is my favorite time of year. The air feels crisp and clean. The changing of the leaves is just around the corner. The days are wonderfully cool. These days feel the best to me. This is the first time in many years that I have remembered just how much I love the fall. Seems the approach of winter reminds me to take full advantage of the remaining warm weather. To live life to it's fullest before I settle in for the winter. Today I am going to leave a little early so I can enjoy my morning cup of coffee outside on the patio and prepare myself for this wonderful day.

Love you all,
Ride the turtle
Phil

A Glimpse of the Journey

September 21, 2012

Good Morning,

Prayer has become an everyday affair for me, most days when I get up and always several times each day. Having the freedom to choose a god of my understanding helps me. I used to have an image of a big white-bearded guy with flowing robes, who judged me for my wrongs. Now my god wears blue jeans, boots, t-shirts and kicks it with the fellas. He likes to smile and laugh and he encourages me when I need it. He loves me when I make mistakes and smirks when I do something foolish, shakes his head when I am a fool and says maybe next time. My God is compassionate and understanding. All that makes it much easier for me to pray.

When I pray to a loving, kind God, the words come easy. So anyway me and my god are heading out to work.

Love you all,
RTT
Phil

Phil Krause

September 23, 2012

Good Morning,

Last night I got off work earlier than I expected and rushed home to find my son off to spend the night at his Mom's house. I wondered what to do, meeting? Coffee? Visit with friends? I took one boot off to scratch my foot and sat on the couch. The last few days of long hours suddenly rushed up and I sat there wrestling with whether to take off the other boot or put the other one back on. Boot off won and I laid down on the couch and suddenly felt very peaceful. This is an unusual feeling, comfortable in my own skin, not needing to be with anyone to feel at ease. A few texts and an evening of quiet time. Feels good not having to chase after the things I used to have to have. Slowly over a period of time, I get better.

Love you all,
RTT
Phil

A Glimpse of the Journey

September 24, 2012

Good Morning,

The only limits to my HP's love, compassion and ability are ones I impose. My HP wants the best for me and is working towards the most wonderful life for me. If I will let him. I have to remember that the gifts I have received so far are far greater than the ones I would have wished for when I first got into recovery. The relationship I have with my loved ones is healthier now than it has ever been and is always improving. My work ethic is better than it has ever been and is improving. My house cleaning skill…..well, ok so there is plenty of room for improvement still. But I am working on it. ☺

Love you all,
RTT
Phil

September 26, 2012

Good Morning,

I have learned in the rooms how to care about others and their feelings. I have learned how to share about mine. I have learned that I am powerless. I have learned that the only person I can change is me. I have learned compassion and empathy, honesty and loyalty. I have learned how to love my friends and how to love myself. I see friends in and out of the program struggling with love. Sex isn't love. Although sometimes love includes sex. Marriage isn't love, although sometimes love includes marriage. Sacrifice isn't love … the list goes on and on. I can love someone with all or none of these things. I do know that the one thing I can't live without is love. Love from the outside in, is important. But love from the inside out, is imperative.

Love you all,
Phil

A Glimpse of the Journey

September 27, 2012

Good Morning,

The support I receive from my friends is one of the most powerful factors in my success at life. Knowing I always have somewhere to turn for encouragement, advice wisdom or just a hug when I need one. My group of friends are some of the huggingest people I know. I always know where to get a hug. I know with the support I have I can make it through anything without using. I can get suggestions on how to approach my problems or at least how not to approach my problems. The willingness to share, the willingness to help, the willingness to be my friends and to love me no matter what. Feels good to have that kind of support and feels even better when I can give that kind of support.

Love you all,
RTT
Phil

September 29, 2012

Good Morning,

If I have a little faith in God and have a little faith in me, it will all be all right. A little prayer and a little gritting my teeth and it will all be fine. My life improves and I find strength when I just have a little faith.

Love you all,
RTT
Phil

October 2012

October 8, 2012

Good Morning,

Leaving old patterns behind, I choose to surround myself with new people, new ideas, new patterns. The people I choose to surround myself with are encouraging. The ideas are positive and the patterns get larger, not progressively smaller. I look outside the circle not inward toward the middle. My base is solid. I have slowly built a foundation for this new life carefully laying the groundwork. Keeping good ideas that work for me and discarding the ones that don't. Seeing the potential in myself and those around me. Allowing myself to like the situations I find myself in. Even the uncomfortable ones. Finding joy in simple things, a sunny day shared with a friend, a cup of coffee on a chilly morning, a smile from a stranger. Gratitude, a god full of grace. Loving life.

Phil

October 13, 2012

Good Morning,

When working long days I get self-centered. I forget to be of service to my fellow man. I forget an act of kindness can go a very long way. Time to get out of myself and perform at least one act of kindness today. One thing, no matter how small will lead to many other good things. So today at least one act of kindness.

Love you all,
Phil

October 14, 2012

Good Morning,

Now through the fellowship of NA, I no longer have to be lonely. I also have the responsibility to my friends that they may never be lonely again as well. I have learned what true friendship is and how to be a good friend. Lots of changing, lots of learning.

October 19, 2012

Good Morning,

I have been feeling myself beginning to isolate. I have been staying in more often. I have been going to meetings. So time to positive up again and get involved. I got no business isolating. I have been losing my enthusiasm for work. Time to nip that in the butt as well. I enjoy my work. I enjoy the people I meet and the things I see and learn about others. For the most part, people are generous and kind. It's time for me to be enthusiastic about my work and my recovery again.

Love you all,
Phil

A Glimpse of the Journey

October 26, 2012

Good Morning,

First of all they finally replaced my phone with a new one. If you are getting this I still have your number. Please tell our friends to contact me so I can put them in my phone again.

I was woken last night by a nightmare, a terrible monster was destroying everything in sight, seeking revenge against everyone, hurting people I care about with no regard for human life or emotions. There were instances of violence, rage and intimidation. It scared the hell out of me when I realized I was seeing all if it from the monster's point of view. I laid awake for a few hours tossing and turning wondering how the circumstances could have been different. When I realized it all could have been avoided had I changed the monster, not the circumstances around the monster. No change = no change. Change the beast within. Do that through the program.

Love you all,
Phil

October 27, 2012

Good Morning,

These feelings of having lost my enthusiasm for work are not unfamiliar to me. I have had these feelings with jobs before. In the past these feelings usually led to a job change. My past does not have to rule my future. The job I have is a blessing. Many are without work and I am not one of them. I enjoy what I do and enjoy the environment I do it in. So time to put on my big boy undies and sling on my tool belt and go do my job. My job, that needs to be said with a feeling pride.

Hope you have a wonderful Day.
I plan on having one.

Love you all,
Phil

A Glimpse of the Journey

October 29, 2012

Good Morning,

This morning early I woke up to the ache, cough and low-grade fever that comes with the first respiratory infection of the season. My first thought was ouch, but my second thought was this is the first time in over 33 years that I will face one of these without smoking. Shouldn't last as long, should help clear all that yuck of smoking from my lungs and I won't hurt as bad going through it. Perspective ....

Love you all,
Phil

November 2012

November 14, 2012

Good Morning,

If I could plot a graph of life improvement for addicts in recovery (improvement of life over time), how do you think it would look? I know my personal graph would be through the roof in many areas and every area of my life would have upward trends to it. I hadn't really thought about it but there are no areas in my life that have not improved since my clean date. There have been sections of time when growth has slowed, but always there has been growth. When I was using I had to go to a dealer, one I could see and usually the dope was good, but not always. In my recovery I have to go to a dealer and this dope is always good.

My go to dealer is NA and I think I will keep coming back.

Love you all,
Phil

A Glimpse of the Journey

November 15, 2012

Good Morning,

There is not point in living a frantic existence! Wow ... why am I still always in a hurry? I was so excited when I realized I was taking the time to enjoy the sunrise and sunsets. I forget there is beauty all around me all the time. Sometimes it's the scenery outside the car. Sometimes it's acts of kindness. Sometimes it's people taking the risk to confront a friend about something that makes them uncomfortable. Sometimes.... when I'm lucky, it's sitting in the passenger seat. ;-). But I digress. Lol. Today I think I will recognize the beauty all around me.

Love you all,
Phil

November 22, 2012

Happy Thanksgiving,

Today I give thanks for each and everyone of you. Without you I would be just an addict. With you I am an addict in recovery. I can't, we can. You, my dear friends are one of the corner stones in my recovery and I love each and every one of you. And there ain't nothing you can do about it.

Phil

December 2012

December 3, 2012

Good Morning,

Through some trials and tribulations this weekend I learned many things. Among them is that I teach people how to treat me. I get to decide what is acceptable in my life and what is not acceptable. I cannot change anyone else. I can change my proximity to them however. This past month has been one of little work and much play. Today, that all changes. And it's back to the regular life. I look forward to getting back to the norm of a while. There is peace in the day-to-day life of work. There is a certain stability there that I have come to appreciate. It tends to cut into my meeting time. But it is a balance.

Love you all,
Phil

December 7

Good Morning,

I went home Tuesday, sick. I missed three days of work and received a text Thursday afternoon that said, "no work for you tomorrow." I immediately went to Oh no I'm fired, my job gone, what will I do. I called my boss and asked what was up. They needed three guys off the load and because I had been sick he put me on the list. I have to admit I am a bit concerned. So I pray. I look logically at the situation. I spoke honestly with my boss who reassured me my job was no more on the line than anyone else's. In the past I would start the sabotage. I would find a reason to quit before they could fire me. My emotions used to rule my life. But if I am not willing to try something new, my life would never change. I think I will practice the principles of the program, use the tools of this new life to overcome the old me.

Love you all,

Phil

A Glimpse of the Journey

December 11, 2012

Good Morning,

My life used to be run by my emotions and my misery, then I realized they were one and the same. I choose to be happy or sad. I choose happy today.

Love you all,
Phil

December 12, 2012

Good Morning,

Yesterday my ex sent me a text that my daughter would be staying the night with me. When I replied that was good and I was a excited and always enjoyed her company, I got in return a nasty text about how the only time Bailey stayed here was when I was gone and that I should not have a 16 year old house sitting for me. Now a little over 2 years ago the laundry list of things she could have sent to me about the things I was doing wrong would have filled several pages of text. Today the best she has is that I shouldn't have a 16 year-old house sitting. Progress, not perfection. Sounds like to me I am making some progress.

Thanks for the compliment.
Lol.

Love you all,
Phil

A Glimpse of the Journey

Merry Christmas,

Today I will do something for someone else. Giving of my time, the most precious of gifts.

Love you all,
Phil

January 2013

January 15, 2013

Good Morning,

First of 2 days off. It feels very good to not be bundled up like the kid on 'A Christmas Story', to be warm for a couple of days. To face the extreme dangers of my living room and maybe a grocery store is very appealing. No longer scared to live a life. No longer afraid to interact with society. I still have fears, but they no longer paralyze me. They inspire me to grow and to face them with logic and reason. I choose my friends by how they treat me, not by what I need from them. I choose what I do by what I need to do, not by what I have to do. I am no longer bound by the ropes of addiction.

Love you all,
Phil

A Glimpse of the Journey

January 25, 2013

Good Morning,

I didn't sleep well last night. I have had several things on my mind lately. Being the best man I can be, doing the right thing, praying for the knowledge to do the right thing. I remember coming into the rooms scared and alone. Not knowing what was right, knowing only what was wrong and being very good at it. I may not be the best at knowing and doing what's right. But I am a hell of a lot better than what I was when I got here. I really do enjoy seeing people improve, seeing their lives change, including my own. Thank you god for allowing me the conscience to worry, to know that the consequences of my actions can be far reaching and that I have a responsibility to think before I act.

Love you all,
Phil

January 28, 2013

Good Morning,

Today I get to go to the VA and have my health checked. Things I did not do before, I get to do now. I get to find out if I am healthy or not. I used to worry that I was sick….. now I know I am…..but I go to meetings for that. I look after myself now semi annual check ups, regular meeting attendance. A daily inventory. My physical health, my mental wellbeing are now a priority. So today I will smile when the Dr. tells me to turn my head and cough, and I will do my best to remember how fortunate I am when tells me to bend over … relax … you may feel a little discomfort.

February 2013

February 5, 2013

Good Morning,

Walked in to our first meeting? Half drug in by my heels. But after that, some days I ran into the rooms. The look on some of your faces. That sense of peace I saw on your faces, the confidence you seemed to have when I felt very lost. I wanted what you had … and still do. Make a great day.

Phil Krause

February 7, 2013

Good Morning,

I believe that my HP is not the source of my trouble, my trials or my tribulations. Almost all of those can in some way be attributed to my actions and a few to the actions of others. My HP, my friends and my program are the thing I lean on when life on life's terms sucks. My capacity to act better and my reactions constantly improve with time. A regression now and again when I forget a lesson I have learned or it is time to learn a new one. Progress not perfection.

Love ya all,
Phil
RTT

A Glimpse of the Journey

February 8, 2013

Good Morning,

The other day I called my sponsor with a question about what to do in a certain situation. He said, "wow, you sure do come up with some doozies." And the reality of that is with his guidance, with his patient loving hand on my shoulder for the past tow years, I have begun to trust my own judgment again. I have begun to know the right thing when dealing with some of life's day to day obstacles. I call him on the ones that baffle me. Through the program and approaching life through the steps, I am beginning to have acceptable actions.

Thanks Patrick.

Love you all,
RTT
Phil

February 9, 2013

Thanks to all of you for your help and guidance. Without all of you, I would not have made 1 year with the same company. Me…a year…..with the same job. Hmmmmm who'da thunk it.

Phil Krause

Made in the USA
Charleston, SC
09 November 2014